It's another Quality Book from CGP

This book is for anyone doing GCSE English at Foundation Level.

Whatever subject you're doing it's the same old story — there are lots of facts and you've just got to learn them. GCSE English is no different.

Happily this CGP book gives you all that important information as clearly and concisely as possible.

It's also got some daft bits in to try and make the whole experience at least vaguely entertaining for you.

What CGP is all about

Our sole aim here at CGP is to produce the highest quality books — carefully written, immaculately presented and dangerously close to being funny.

Then we work our socks off to get them out to you — at the cheapest possible prices.

CONTENTS

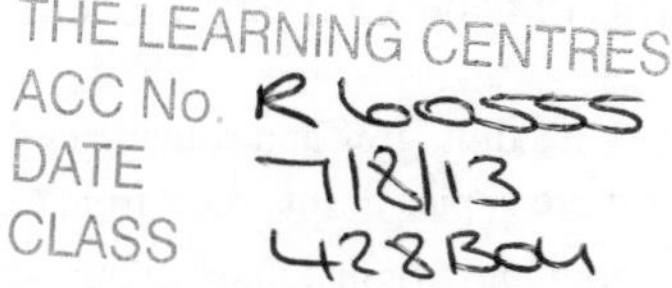

Published by CGP

Editors:
Claire Boulter
Heather Gregson
Luke von Kotze
Rachael Powers

Contributors:
Tony Flanagan
Ian Miles

With thanks to Polly Cotterill and Nicola Woodfin for the proofreading.

ISBN: 978 1 84762 577 9

Groovy website: www.cgpbooks.co.uk
Jolly bits of clipart from CorelDRAW®
Printed by Elanders Ltd, Newcastle upon Tyne.

Based on the classic CGP style created by Richard Parsons.

What You Have to Do

GCSE English exams — yep, they're on their way. But they're not as scary as you think.

What you Have to Do depends on Which Route you take

There are two ways to study English at GCSE nowadays. You can take either:

ENGLISH LANGUAGE

AND

ENGLISH LITERATURE

= 2 GCSEs

OR

ENGLISH

= 1 GCSE

(which is mainly English Language, but has a bit of Literature thrown in for fun)

Your teacher should be able to tell you which route you're taking.

You'll be Assessed in two Different Ways

Those little devils at the exam board have got two ways of assessing you:

1) CONTROLLED ASSESSMENT  You'll have to do a set of tasks in class, under exam-like conditions.

2) EXAMS

Your GCSE(s) will be split into different units of work. You'll have to do either an exam or controlled assessment for each unit.

What you'll be doing for GCSE English

Every exam board is different, so check with your teacher to find out exactly what you'll have to do for your GCSE English. It'll probably involve some of these things:

- Answering questions about unseen non-fiction texts.
- Writing your own pieces of non-fiction writing.
- Doing some creative writing.
- Responding to some literary texts (one by Shakespeare, one from a different culture and one from the English Literary Heritage, i.e. an old book or poem).
- Completing a series of speaking and listening tasks.

Let's talk about exams baby, let's talk about you and me...

So this page covers the info for GCSE English. BUT if you're studying English Language and English Literature, you'll need to read the next page. Go on, turn the page. Don't be scared. Go on...

What You Have to Do

Aren't you glad you turned the page? This page covers English Language and English Literature.

What you'll be doing for GCSE English Language

English Language is mainly about your own writing, non-fiction texts and speaking and listening.
The way you're examined will depend on the exam board, so check with your teacher.
It'll probably involve some of these things:

- Answering questions about some unseen non-fiction texts.
- Writing your own pieces of non-fiction writing.
- Doing some creative writing.
- Reading and writing about an extended text.
- Carrying out a study on spoken language.
- Completing a series of speaking and listening tasks.

Some of these are exactly the same as GCSE English.

English Literature is a bit more Complicated

1) There are different units in English Literature for each exam board.
2) You'll have to study a wide range of texts for each exam board — a mixture of poetry, prose and drama, which might include:

- a Shakespeare play
- prose from a different culture
- contemporary (modern) drama or prose
- drama or prose from the English, Irish or Welsh literary heritage
- poetry

3) You'll have a combination of exams and controlled assessments.
4) You might have an exam question on an unseen poem — this will be a poem that you haven't come across before or studied in class.

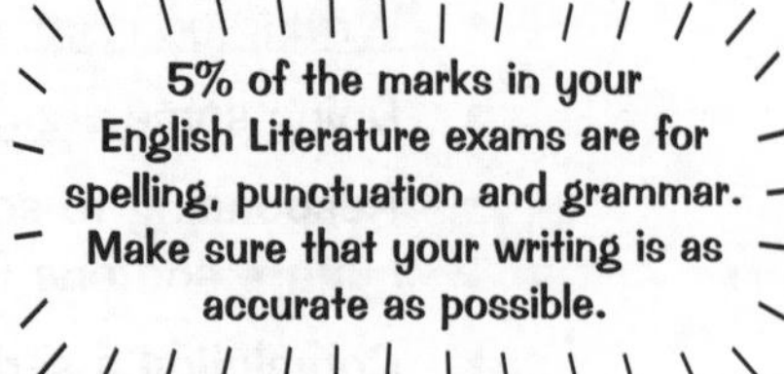

5% of the marks in your English Literature exams are for spelling, punctuation and grammar. Make sure that your writing is as accurate as possible.

Talk about the prose and cons of GCSE English Literature...

I know, I know, it's a lot to take in. Ask your teacher if you're not sure whether you're doing Language and Literature or GCSE English. Then settle down to enjoy the rest of this book.

Planning

You've got to make a plan for every essay you write. That's a plan on paper — not in your head.

Decide what to say Before you start Writing

Think about what you're going to write before you start — that way your ideas will have a clear structure.

Good writing makes a point. It doesn't just ramble on about nothing.

In an exam, try to come up with enough ideas to keep you writing till your time's up.

Don't forget to leave yourself about 5 minutes to check through your work though.

Stick your Points down on Paper

1) Jot down a plan of the points you want to make before you start writing.
2) Don't bother writing your plan in proper sentences — it's a waste of time.
3) In the exams spend (roughly) 5 MINUTES planning every answer.

Q1 A local nature reserve is looking for part-time volunteers to help them out during the summer holidays. You decide to apply. Write your letter of application.

Your letter should include:
- who you are
- why you would like to volunteer
- why you think you're right for the job

You'll need to write about all the bullet points if the question has them.

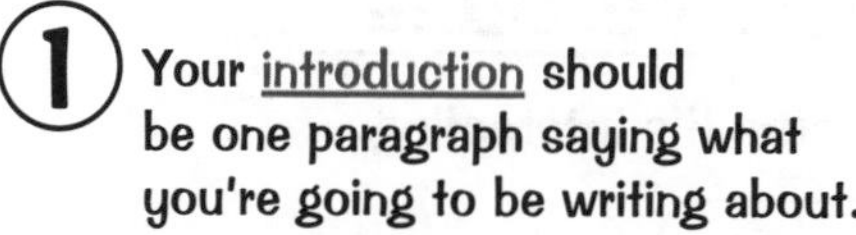

1 Your introduction should be one paragraph saying what you're going to be writing about.

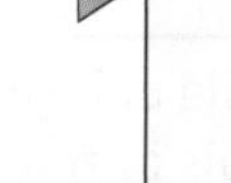

2 Write down the points you want to make. Use examples to back them up.

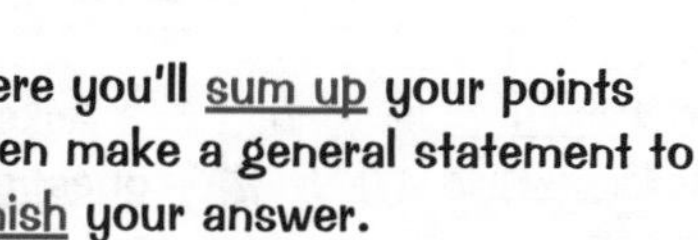

3 Here you'll sum up your points then make a general statement to finish your answer.

INTRODUCTION

— Who you are and reason for letter

DEVELOPMENT

— Why you'd like to volunteer — interested in nature

— Why you think you're right for the job — skills — personal qualities — previous work experience

CONCLUSION

— Available for interview — hope to hear from reserve soon

No rambling — so no walking boots needed...

Writing that rambles on without getting anywhere isn't going to get you good marks. All this needs to be second nature by the time you get to the exam, so get learning.

Starting Your Answer

You need to write a clear and punchy introduction to your answer — no waffle allowed.

Start with a Good Introduction

In your introduction you should introduce the overall point that your essay is making — and do it clearly.

The introduction gives a brief answer to the question. The rest of the essay goes into more depth, and gives evidence to back up your points.

Tell the reader What you're going to Say...

Use your introduction to clearly tell the reader what your essay is about.

1. Compare the texts 'Antipodean Adventures' and 'My Journey Across Australia' using the following headings:
   - the presentation of the text
   - the layout of the text

It makes it easier to answer the question if you use similar wording to the question.

'Antipodean Adventures' and 'My Journey Across Australia' both use presentation and layout for effect. 'Antipodean Adventures' uses bright colours to appeal to younger readers. 'My Journey Across Australia' has a more formal layout to suit its adult audience.

Clear argument.

Use the introduction to Grab the Reader's Attention...

Your first paragraph should make the reader want to read on, so make sure it's interesting.

2. Write an article for a magazine arguing against keeping wild animals in zoos. The article should include:
   - why keeping wild animals in zoos is wrong
   - what should be done about it

Imaginative beginning to interest the reader.

Language appeals to the reader's emotions.

Put yourself in his shoes: you're the king of the jungle — you should be running wild and free. Instead you're pacing a tiny concrete cell with nothing to do but stare at the blank walls. How would you feel? Yes we need to protect endangered animals, but shouldn't we have found a better way?

Asks questions to draw the reader in.

Refers to the opposite point of view.

The intro is important — it's the only bit they actually read... (just kidding)

No, but the introduction is very important — it sets the scene for the whole piece. A really good, attention-grabbing one will make your reader want to read on — a dull one won't.

Paragraphs

Here's a little secret from me to you — use paragraphs properly if you want to get a decent grade.

Paragraphs make your writing Clearer

1) A paragraph is a group of sentences. These sentences are usually about the same thing.
2) You need to start a new paragraph every time there's a change.

> The street was quiet and very dark. Alex walked on tiptoes, trying to make as little noise as possible. He kept wondering what might be lurking around the next corner.
>
> Suddenly Alex heard a faint noise. Could it be the dreaded peanut-butter monster?

The ideas in this paragraph are all about Alex walking down the street. When something new happens, you start a new paragraph.

Start a New Paragraph every time Something Changes

When You Start Writing About a New Place

> The playing fields were quiet and peaceful. There was no one around except Pete.
>
> Further down the valley, a huge cloud of dust rose into the sky.

This is happening somewhere else.

When You Talk About a New Person

> Liam sat on the edge of the stage, thinking about his guitar.
>
> Then he saw Keith. Keith was a skinny, ill-looking boy. He was carrying an enormous guitar case.

This is a new paragraph for a new person.

When You Start Writing About a Different Time

> By five o'clock, Edwin was angry. Shirley was late again, and the flower he'd bought was starting to droop.
>
> Six o'clock came, and still she didn't appear. Enough was enough.

This one's gone forward to a different time.

Each Time a New Person Speaks

> "I'll find him," muttered Donald. "He won't get away this time."
>
> "What makes you so sure?" asked Mickey.

Someone new is speaking.

When You Start Writing About a New Topic

> It's widely known that smoking is bad for your health. It can lead to cancer and an early death.
>
> In addition, smoking is an expensive habit. Cigarette prices rise all the time but people will always pay.

This is another reason why smoking is bad.

It's important to make one clear point in each paragraph.

Changing paragraphs — any time, any place...

Remember, start a new paragraph whenever you change the person speaking, the people, the place or the time. Or whenever you make a new point. Very important that one.

Paragraphs

Once you've got your paragraphs sorted, you've got to make sure they flow properly.

Paragraphs need to be Linked Together

Use words and phrases like these to make the link clear:

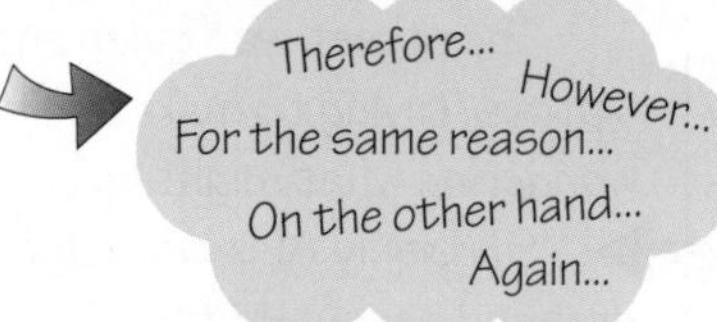

Therefore...
However...
For the same reason...
On the other hand...
Again...

These words link the paragraph's meaning to the one before it:

> ... free school meals for all pupils would mean that everyone got one healthy meal a day.
> However, some people say that free school meals would be too expensive...

> ... people like the Scouts and yoga group use the town hall every week.
> Therefore, I feel it would be a very bad idea to close the town hall...

Paragraphs should Follow a Clear Order

1) Make sure your paragraphs have a clear order.
2) It's up to you how you do it — just make sure it makes sense.

SOME IDEAS

- Put your paragraphs in order of importance.
- Give paragraphs for an argument then paragraphs against.
- Put your paragraphs in time order.

Try to Vary The Style of your paragraphs

You don't want to make all of your paragraphs exactly the same.

Here are a few tips for spicing things up a bit...

You could repeat sentence structures:

> Johnny was glad he was at the farm. At school, he felt like he didn't belong. At home, all he ever seemed to do was get in the way. But at the farm, Johnny came to life.

Or start with a rhetorical question (see p.30):

> Is a world filled with violence and fear really the one we want our children to grow up in?

Paragraphs — they do more than you think...

Paragraphs give structure to your answer and break it into separate points so it's easier to read. Excellent news. You can also use them creatively to make your work that bit more interesting.

Formal and Informal Language

As a general rule, use formal language unless you're writing to friends or young people.

Write in Formal Language

1) You use formal language to speak or write to people you don't know — especially people in charge. This includes your examiner.
2) You should use formal language in most of your essays.
3) When you use formal language, be accurate and to the point. Don't be chatty — that means no slang:

> I reckon Lady Macbeth wore the trousers in that household — she wasn't half bossy towards her old man. ✗

> Lady Macbeth was a forceful character, who had a strong influence over her husband. ✓

And then I want you to clean the cat, then take the cat into the garden and make it dirty, then clean it again. Then you can kill Malcolm for me.

4) You must use correct punctuation, grammar and spelling (see section 9).
5) Don't say "I" this and "I" that — just talk about the question, the text, the characters, the style, etc.

> ~~I think that~~ The language in the poem creates a sad mood. For example, ~~I believe that~~ the image of the white blossom turning brown shows how their love has been ruined.

Only use Informal Language when it Suits The Task

1) You use informal language with friends or people you know well. It's chattier and more relaxed than formal language, but it DOESN'T mean you can use text speak.
2) You'll need to use formal language for most of your work, but sometimes you'll be asked to write in a certain style, e.g. a letter to a friend.
3) Here's an example of the kind of answer you should give if you're asked to write a talk for teenagers about the internet:

Informal language is more suited to this audience than formal language.

> ... I'm not saying the internet isn't useful, but how many hours have you lost watching X-factor hopefuls make fools of themselves on YouTube when you really should be researching your history project?

You still need to use fancy writing tricks to get the marks though. This is a rhetorical question — it doesn't need a reply because the answer should be obvious.

Could you inform Al that I wrote this page for Mal...

So basically, you've almost always got to use formal language in your writing. That means proper spelling, punctuation and grammar and absolutely no slang.

Giving Evidence and Quoting

You have to give evidence for everything you say or you'll miss out on loads of marks.

Give an Example every time you make a Point

You've got to show that you know what you're talking about — and to do that, you've got to give examples for what you write. If you don't, it could look like you're just making things up.

The woman was cruel to her dog.

This answer doesn't give any reasons...

...but this answer gives examples to back up the point it makes. That's loads better.

The woman was cruel to her dog. She kept him chained up in the sun all day, with very little food and no water.

Use Quotes from other people

1) Quoting means using someone else's words to back up your arguments.
2) To quote someone in their own words, put quotation marks (" ") around the quote. This separates the other person's words from yours.

The quotation marks separate your words...

...from Mr. Wright's words.

Mr. Wright claimed that "there was no other possible course of action."

Tips for using quotation marks:

- Use exactly the same words and punctuation as the person you're quoting.
- Don't make the quote too long.

3) If you put something into your own words, you don't need quotation marks:

Mrs. Priya says, "Reading greatly improves vocabulary."

Direct quote

Mrs. Priya claims that a good way to improve vocabulary is through reading.

In your own words

Writing must Flow around Quotes

Put your quotes in so the words around them still make sense and flow well:

Mr Jones said, "Getting children interested in drama is important to us." The board has agreed to pay for the drama workshops.

"Quotes are great," said CGP

If you use loads of good quotes, you'll definitely improve your grade. Just remember, if you're quoting to support a point, explain why your quote backs it up. See page 14 for more about this.

Concluding

You've got to conclude your answer — but it shouldn't be a last-minute rushed job.

Bring together the Key Points in your Conclusion

You need to be able to finish off your essay properly — and that means writing a good conclusion.

Q. Write an article for a student magazine explaining why backpacking is popular as a form of travel.

1) Start a new paragraph by going back to the question.

2) Go over the main points of your answer. Don't add any new points. They should be in the main part of your essay.

> For many people, backpacking is the best way to travel round different countries. It lets you travel wherever you want, and it's great for meeting interesting people. It is also the cheapest way of travelling, so people are more likely to be able to afford a visit to places that are far away. It's good to know that people don't need all their luxuries when they travel.

3) Once you've summed up, write one last sentence to finish.

There are lots of Different Kinds of Conclusion

1) You could give advice about what to do next.

> ... we must do something. We need to create more protected areas of woodland before it's too late.

2) You could ask the reader a rhetorical question (see p.30).

> ... so, do we take action or just sit back and do nothing? Is this the end of the world as we know it?

This gives the reader a chance to make up their own mind.

3) You could go back to the points you made in your introduction — it shows you've planned your work.

4) If you're writing using formal language, you could start your last paragraph with 'In conclusion...'. That way, the examiner knows that you're wrapping up your essay.

Is this page important? Draw your own conclusions...

Oh wow, what a great page. It's one major tip-fest. I know you probably want to just read it again and again, but there's still one last page of this ace section waiting for you. Ooh, you jammy sausage.

Checking

You've got five minutes left in the exam... time to read through your work.

Check Over your Essay when you've Finished

1) Check the grammar, spelling and punctuation. If you find a mistake, put brackets round it, cross it out neatly with two lines through it and write the correction above.

2) If you've written something which isn't clear, put a star * at the end of the sentence. Put another star at the end of your answer, and write what you mean beside it.

* something I forgot

3) If you realise you should have started a new paragraph, put "//" to show where it starts.

4) If you find you've missed out a word or two, put one of these: "∧" where the words should go, then write them in above the line.

Don't Panic if you realise you've Gone Wrong in an Exam

If you realise you've forgotten something obvious, then add it in — even if it's at the bottom of the final page. You might get marks for noticing your mistake.

Never cross out your whole answer if you realise it's wrong. If you've got time left, explain what the real answer is.

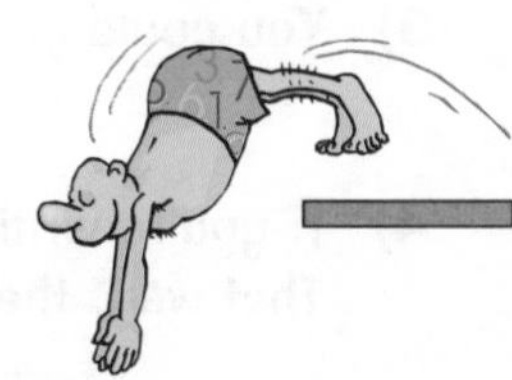

Roger had forgotten something obvious.

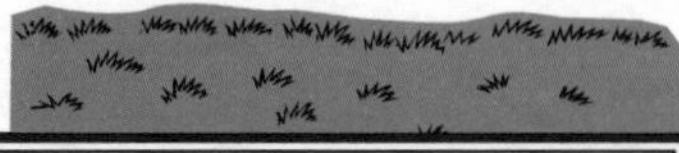

Alweys chck yoor worke

Mistakes are easy to make, especially in exam conditions, so you must give yourself time to check things over. Don't panic if you've gone wrong — there are plenty of ways to fix it.

Revision Summary

Every now and then throughout this book, you'll find pages like this one.
They may look dull, but they're really important, so don't skip them.

You've read the section, but do you know it? Here's where you find out — right here, right now.

Do all these questions without cheating, then turn back and look up the bits you didn't know.
Check them, and do the whole lot again until you get 100% correct.

1) How long (roughly) should you spend planning each exam answer?
2) Your plan should cover the main three sections of your answer. The first of these sections is the introduction. What are the other two?
3) What should your introduction tell the reader?
4) How might your introduction grab the reader's attention?
5) Why should you write your answers using paragraphs?
6) Which of these would be a reason to start a new paragraph — a) when a new person speaks, b) when you write about a new place or a new time, c) when you're hungry?
7) Which of these words and phrases are generally good for linking paragraphs — a) However, b) I don't know, c) On the other hand, d) Horses?
8) Which would be better — to order your paragraphs from longest to shortest or in order of importance?
9) Give an example of how you could vary the style of your paragraphs.
10) What does 'formal writing' mean?
11) Which of the following would you write in informal language — a) a letter to your MP, b) a postcard to your friend, c) an article on clothes for a teenage magazine?
12) Why do you need to give examples for the points you make?
13) Do you need quotation marks when you put what someone else has said into your own words?
14) Which of these would make a good conclusion — a) advice about what to do next, b) a brand new point, c) go over the points you made in your introduction, d) your reader's horoscope?
15) Explain why you need to leave yourself time at the end of the exam to check through your answer.
16) What's the best thing to do if you realise that you've forgotten to include something important in your exam answer?

Reading The Questions

A non-fiction text is anything that's about real life, like a newspaper article or a leaflet.

Three Things to get you Marks in Non-Fiction Text exams

These are all things that the examiner wants to give you marks for:

If you're doing Edexcel, non-fiction texts could be part of a controlled assessment or an exam.

1. Showing that you've understood and thought about the texts, and that you can compare them.
2. Showing that you can pick out facts from the text and explain them.
3. Explaining how language and how the text looks can influence the reader.

Read the Question Before the Text

Look at the question before you start — it'll tell you what to look out for.

Pick out the key words in each question. Underline them, so you can see at a glance what the main point of each one is.

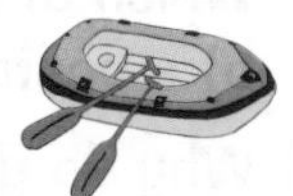

We should have started building this much earlier...

1 Compare how the writers use language to influence the reader in 'The Future of Our Planet: Should We Be Building an Ark?' and 'End of the World? I don't think so.'

Think about How Much the question is Worth

1) The questions are worth different amounts of marks. The number of marks for each question will be written on the exam paper.
2) Make sure you know what the total number of marks is. Then you can decide how much of the total time to spend on each question.
3) Don't spend half the exam answering a question worth 4 marks if the next question's worth 8 marks.

What's the question worth? — I'll give you £5 and a lemon bonbon...

Spend less time on questions that are worth fewer marks — simple really. And remember, what the examiner really wants is for you to show you've understood the text. Do that and you're laughing.

Reading The Text And Making Notes

No one likes making notes, but they stop you rambling on in your essays like a rambly thing.

You might need to Pick Out Facts from the text

Questions which ask you to pick out facts only need short answers.

1) A question may ask you to find and write down some bits of information from the text.
2) Read the question really carefully and only write down things the question asks for.
3) Look at the number of marks the question is worth. This should tell you how many facts you need to pick out in your answer.

Find the bits that Answer the Question

After you've read the question, go through each text at least twice, slowly and carefully.

1 What are the writer's thoughts and feelings towards Ben Kilham's approach?
Your answer should include:
- whether or not he agrees with it
- what other people think
- his overall impression.

GENTLE BEN

Most people try not to get too close to wild bears. Not Ben Kilham. When two injured bears were brought to his animal park, he brought them home and looked after them in his guest room. "It didn't take long for them to trust me," he says, "They used to follow me round the house." Some experts worry that treating bears this way will make them too tame. However, Kilham cared for three cubs last year and they now live happily in the animal park with the other bears.

Key point — Includes Ben's own words — shows the writer thinks what Ben says is important and suggests he agrees with him.

Key point — Shows what other people think about Ben's approach.

Key point — The writer provides another argument which supports Ben's approach.

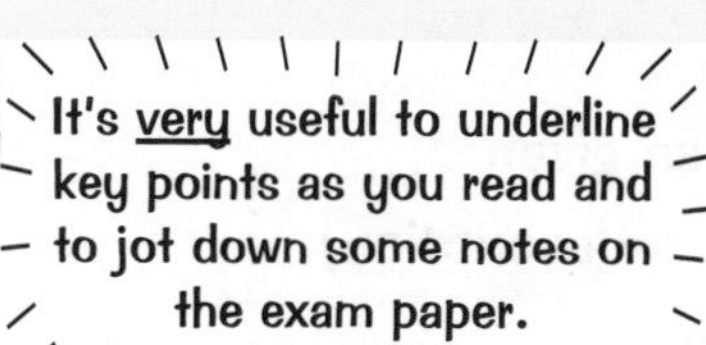

It's very useful to underline key points as you read and to jot down some notes on the exam paper.

If I said I was a little bear would you hold it against me...

The examiners want to know you've understood the text. When you're picking points out, make sure you're only writing down things that the question asks for. Anything else is just a waste of time.

Longer Answers

The next two pages will give you the wicked skills to write longer, more detailed answers.

Try to sound Confident

Use your own words to explain the question and then say what your argument's going to be.

2 How does the writer of 'Careless Talk' use language to make the article informative and interesting?

Key words.

This is dull — it just repeats the question.

'Careless Talk' is informative and interesting because of the language used.

This is much better.

'Careless Talk uses quotes and stories from real people to inform the reader and keep them interested.

Back up your points with Examples

1) For questions that ask for longer answers, you'll need to back up your points with evidence.
2) This will usually be a quote (see p.8), but it could be a description of the pictures or layout.
3) It's important to explain what your example shows about the text.

These examples are about the presentation of the text.

The leaflet is designed to appeal to young children.
For example, it uses bright colours and simple fonts.
This makes the leaflet look friendly and fun.

This explains why the writer chose a certain style.

So, here's what a good essay answer should do:

1) Make points to answer the question you've been given.
2) Give examples from the text (either a quote or a description).
3) Explain how your examples back up your point.

Don't bury examiners with lots of detail — use soil...

OK, so you get the message — confident, uncluttered, own words... Lovely. The thing about examiners is that they can spot a load of waffle a mile off so stick to the point.

Longer Answers

There are plenty of ways you can develop your answer — there's more to it than adding quotes.

Some questions ask about Thoughts and Feelings

You may understand the facts a writer gives you, but some questions will ask for more.

1) Try to work out how the writer feels about what they're describing. For example:

> There is a strong sense that the writer feels angry about the changes.

2) You could show you understand what the writer wants readers to think about. For example:

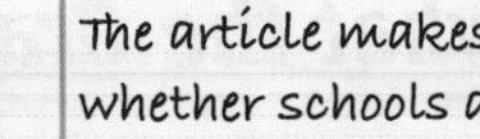

> The article makes the reader question whether schools are a good thing.

3) You could comment on how the writer tries to make readers feel. For example:

> The writer seems to want to make readers feel guilty.

Some questions will ask about the writer's language — make sure you read section 3 to see the kind of techniques that you'll need to look out for.

Compare and Contrast the texts

1) You might get a question asking you to compare the bits of text you're given. That means picking out the differences and similarities between them.

2) The question could give you some headings to help you compare the texts. Make sure you write about all of these headings and write about the same amount for each one.

3) Always plan your answer before you start. If you've been given headings, include points about each one in your plan.

4) Try to write an equal amount about both texts. Keep making links between them in your answer.

Never trust a mouse to plan your work. I did and look what happened.

English and chocolate cake — compare and contrast

The take-home message here (besides the fact that English and cake have very little in common) is that you need to think beyond the obvious and consider things like the writer's thoughts and ideas.

Writing About The Format of a Non-Fiction Text

There's lots to think about when it comes to non-fiction texts — it's not all about the words.

It's Not Just Words you need to think about

1) The texts in the exam could be magazine or newspaper articles, or printed adverts.
2) You need to comment on the format of what you're given — think about things like the overall presentation, the layout of the text and the way graphics are used.

'Format' means the way the writing and pictures are organised to make a text look.

Think about what the Graphics are trying to Do

1) Texts often have graphics, e.g. photos, pictures, diagrams.
2) They might have captions with them — a short bit of text to explain what the graphic shows.
3) All graphics have a purpose, e.g. photos can show real-life examples of what's in the text, charts show information clearly.

Mention the Layout

Different layouts are used for different audiences.

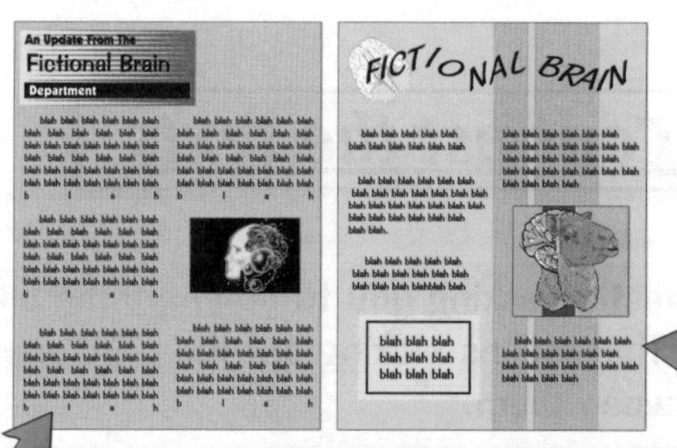

This layout is serious. There's hardly any colour, most of the text is the same size and the picture is formal. It's probably aimed at adults.

This layout is more fun. There's lots of colour, more space, the text size is varied, the picture is more entertaining. It's aimed at young people.

Talk about Headlines too

1) Headlines tell you what the article is about in a few words. They're there to grab your interest, so you'll read the article.
2) Headlines are usually bigger and at the top of the page.
3) They can use humour or shocking facts to get your attention.

This is the headline.

Secret Exam Shocker — 'Revision Works' Says Student

Graphics will pop up all the time, so just use your common sense to explain what you can see. Think about what kind of graphic it is, why you think it's there and the effect it has.

Revision Summary

Non-fiction texts don't have to be tricky. Just remember to read them with the question in mind so you know what to look out for. That way you can underline the key points and it'll be a breeze when you come to writing the answer.

You know the drill, anyway. If you can get through these questions okay, you'll be just about ready to take on the world...

1) Why should you read the question before the text?
2) Is there any point in thinking about how many marks a question is worth? Why?
3) Explain why it's important to read through the question slowly and make a few notes before you start thinking about how to start your essay.
4) If a question asks you to pick out some facts from the text, why is it important to look at the number of marks the question is worth?
5) What kind of first impression do you want your answer to make on the examiner?
6) When you make a point in an essay, what should you back it up with?
   a) nothing — you don't have the time
   b) examples from the text
   c) a comfortable cushion
7) Other than facts, what else could you think about when writing about a text?
   a) how the writer feels about the subject
   b) what you think they had for breakfast
   c) what the writer wants the reader to think about
8) If you're asked to compare and contrast, what should you do?
   a) write about the similarities and differences between the texts
   b) just write about one text in detail and ignore the other one
   c) rock back and forward on your chair in a mad panic
9) What is meant by the 'format' of a text?
10) List three different kinds of graphics that you might find in a non-fiction text.
11) What is the purpose of a caption?
12) Is it important to think about the layout of a non-fiction text? Why?
13) What is the main purpose of a headline?

Different Forms

Non-fiction texts come in many different forms. The next two pages cover the main ones.

Letters can be Formal or Informal

1) Informal letters are the kind of letters that you'd send to a friend.
   You can use a chatty style if it suits the reader, but stick to Standard English (see p.67).
2) Formal letters, e.g. job applications, need a more serious tone and language.
3) Give letters a clear structure.
4) Letters can have many different purposes (see p.21). For example, they can be:

- informative — gives the reader information e.g. a letter to a local newspaper telling readers about a fund-raising event.
- persuasive — getting someone to do something e.g. a letter to a friend to persuade them to run a marathon with you.

Newspaper and Magazine articles should be Factual

For newspaper or magazine articles, you only need to write the text, so don't worry about layout.

1) You need to report the facts and give evidence for them — e.g. quotes and statistics (see p.8).
2) Use headlines and subheadings to break up the writing into clear sections.
3) The purpose of an article depends on the type of newspaper/magazine, for example:

- informing — e.g. a newspaper article telling people of the facts about climate change.
- explaining — e.g. a car magazine might explain the features of a new family car.

Leaflets are usually short

Leaflets can be used to inform, advise or put across an argument.

1) If you're writing the text for a leaflet, don't spend time on the layout.
2) Leaflets should catch people's attention and give information as clearly as possible.
   You could use headings and bullet points to break things up.

I'll keep this short and sweet — revise...

Letters, newspaper articles and leaflets can be about almost anything. If you have to write one of these texts in the exam, read the question carefully to find out who you're writing for, and why.

Different Forms

You want more types of non-fiction text? You've come to the right place.

Reviews are Round-Ups of information

See p.32 for more on reviews

Reviews describe something, e.g. a film, and say what is (or isn't) great about it.

1) Reviews can be formal or informal. Their purpose is to inform (see p.27) and give an opinion.
2) Include some facts — your audience needs to know exactly what it is you're writing about.
3) Write confidently. Show your audience that you know what you're talking about.

Talks and Speeches are designed to be Spoken

For talks or speeches, your audience won't have the words written down so you need to make them easy to remember.

1) Make sure you write in a style that would sound good to a room full of listeners.
2) The tone might be formal or informal (see p.7), depending on your audience.
3) You should include some interesting language and techniques (see p.30).
4) Speeches should have a clear structure, e.g. start with a short introduction to your topic and finish by reminding the audience what they've just been told.

Make your writing Organised and Interesting

Whatever form of text you're writing, you'll be marked on:

- how well you organise and communicate the information.
- the quality of your writing.

1) Structure your writing using paragraphs and link your sentences together.
2) Sometimes you can you use things like headings and bullet points (see p.28), but always use paragraphs for the main parts of your text.
3) Always write in a way that'll interest your readers.

Speeches are designed to be spoken — not sung...

For any non-fiction text, the most important things to keep in mind are the purpose of the text and the audience you're writing it for. There's more advice on the next few pages.

Audience

Whatever type of text you're writing, it's vital to keep in mind who you're writing for.

Think about who your Audience is

In exam questions, you may only be given vague information — you'll have to decide on the details.

1) Who are you writing for? You'll usually be given some idea of who your audience is:

- A manager of a business. You might be trying to persuade them to employ you, so use formal language to make yourself sound professional.

- A friend. You can be a bit more laid-back with your friends, but don't overdo it.

- A teenage audience. Your readers will be your age, but don't be too informal.

- An adult audience. Be more formal with adults than you would with younger people.

2) Sometimes you won't get much detail about your audience. In this case, write for a general audience — i.e. not too technical or too informal.
3) Make sure you match the content of your writing to your audience. Choose details that your audience can relate to and which will interest them.

Don't make Informal writing Too Simple

1) If the question asks you to write to a friend, don't write too casually and never use text speak.
2) You can sound chatty but make sure you still include a range of sentences and vocabulary.
3) You can be sarcastic or humorous to make your writing more interesting.

E.g. if you have to write a letter to a friend about being in Year 11, this is the sort of thing you should write:

> *Of course I'm grateful that they allow me to slave tirelessly into the early hours of the morning.*

You've been a wonderful audience...

If you're writing to a friend, make sure you don't write something like "Mate, here's some goss 4 ya. That guy from skool u like stank like 2 much BO basher 2day." The examiners really hate that.

Purpose

Every piece of writing should have a purpose...

Make sure your writing Achieves its Purpose

Some questions have more than one purpose.

1) The purpose tells you how your writing should affect your reader.
2) Common examples of purpose include:

Arguing, persuading... see p.22-26

... informing, explaining, advising... see p.27-29

and describing. see p.37

Exam questions will often give you a big hint about the purpose of the piece. For example:

Write a letter to a local business arguing that schools need more support and persuading them to help.

Write a letter explaining what you do to represent your school at local youth group meetings.

3) Think about the purpose of your writing when you're planning.
If your question has bullet points, make sure you cover all of them.

4) When you've finished writing, read through it again and make sure the purpose of your answer is clear all the way through.

I'd like to work in a bank because I'm good with money...

E.g. If you're applying for a job, have you informed the reader of your talents, and persuaded them that you're the right person to employ?

Choose the right Language for the purpose

The language you use has to suit your purpose.

1) For example, a letter to the council should be formal and serious...
2) ... but an advert for spot cream aimed at teenagers can be chatty and fun.
3) No matter what you're writing though, you need to use a range of vocabulary.
4) It's also worth using lots of detail to suit your purpose. E.g. if you're writing to persuade, you could include some shocking statistics. If you're writing to describe, put in details from all five senses (see p.37).

I'd argue that it's time for an informative explanation...

Before you start writing, make sure you know the purpose of the piece. If you get it wrong and start persuading when you're supposed to be informing, you won't get the best marks.

Persuasive Writing — Structuring Your Answer

You need a good argument and truckloads of evidence to persuade your readers to agree with you.

Make sure your writing is Structured

1) Work out a plan — spend about five minutes making a plan like the one below.
2) Don't keep repeating the same idea — use the bullet points (if you're given some in the question) to organise your ideas clearly.
3) Fill in the gaps — once you've planned, try to fit in bits of evidence, facts, examples etc.

Plan your persuasive answers around this Basic Structure

General Structure	Example Plan
Introduction — Make it clear what you're writing about and what your point of view is.	Save money and the environment by using wind power.
Logical argument — Backed up with facts.	Emphasise how much money it will save.
Emotional argument — Backed up with real-life examples and quotes.	Much better for the environment. Use quotes and figures about problems with fossil fuels.
Other points of view — Why might people disagree with your point of view and how could you convince them you're right?	Expensive to set up, but costs made back within two years.
Conclusion — Summarise your main points.	Saves money and better for the environment. Could end "It's up to you — would you rather destroy the environment or create less pollution?"

I love it when a plan comes together...

Plan what to write, and write what you planned. And remember, if you don't know any facts about the subject you're writing about, you can make them up. Try to make them sound realistic though.

Arguing or Persuading

This page contains a few cunning tricks that you can use to make your writing persuasive.

Use Reason to make your argument Logical

Your argument must make sense.

1) Show the reader that what you're arguing is the only reasonable point of view.
2) You don't have to agree with what you write. Just make sure you have a strong argument.
3) Use definite language (e.g. 'will', 'all').

If you're unhappy about the way farm animals are treated, becoming vegetarian isn't the answer. Buying organic meat is a way of supporting farmers who treat their animals well.

Definite language makes answer sound logical.

Add Emotion for Emphasis

1) Use strong language to show how you feel and to make the reader feel the same way.
2) Don't rely on emotion alone. Always start with a sensible argument and emphasise it with emotion.

If we don't act now, our rivers will be nothing more than dirty sludge. Our children won't know what it's like to paddle in fresh, clear water.

Emotional language makes readers feel guilty about destroying the environment.

Say if you Believe something is Right or Wrong

1) Most people share certain beliefs about things that are right and wrong, e.g. 'poverty is bad'.
2) They tend to feel strongly about these things, so it's often a good idea to use them in your argument.
3) If you mention these things, the reader will also be on your side.
4) For example, you could say:

Logic — I pink therefore I ham...

Tug at people's heartstrings and they'll be putty in your hands. It's the oldest trick in the book. But don't get carried away — the moment you stop being realistic, you've lost them.

Arguing or Persuading

In persuasive writing, make sure you back up your arguments with facts, opinions and examples.

Use facts Carefully

1) Don't get bogged down in statistics, especially in speeches.
2) Use simple, easy-to-understand facts.

Using the Kid800 Wonderpen, 83% of children aged 7 years old wrote an average of 95 words at a speed of 1.58 words per minute..

Confusing — too much detail.

83% of children could write more quickly when using the Kid800 Wonderpen..

This is a good statistic, because it's easy to understand.

Use Opinions from Experts

1) Use expert opinion to back up your arguments.
2) Say who the experts are and how they're related to your argument.
3) You can include expert opinions as quotes (see example below) or as part of the text (see p.8).

Two-thirds of all dragons don't really exist.
Uh oh.

Use Relevant Quotations

Officer Robert Jones agrees, saying, "I've looked into these recent accidents and I can confirm they were all caused by bad weather."

1) Make sure the quote is relevant.
2) Keep it short. Don't include long extracts.
3) Use quotation marks for direct (exact word) quotations and also say who you're quoting.

Use 'Real-life' Examples

1) Your argument should sound as though it's true in real-life.
2) Give examples that sound realistic to make your argument more convincing.
3) Choose examples that fit your argument as closely as possible.

After initial concerns, a skate park was built within the main park. Youth crime has since dropped. This was a direct result of the park, according to local police officer Rose Leven.

I know it's true — I made it up myself...

Use good quotes that will stick in people's minds, but remember that any quotes you make up must be realistic — don't quote an expert saying the world is made of soap.

Think About Your Audience

Keep your reader's point of view in mind when you write, and grab yourself some juicy marks...

Put yourself in the Reader's (or Listener's) Shoes

1) Any piece of writing is going to be read or heard by someone — so you should suit your writing to the reader or audience.
2) To do this, you need to try to guess what your reader's reactions might be...

Think about what the reader Cares About

Think about any concerns the reader might have, and then:

1) Make their concerns sound reasonable.
2) Let them know that you've thought about their concerns.
3) Tell them how your argument addresses their concerns.

A worry that people may have is the amount of litter after the concert. We will have a team working through the night to clear the area by the next morning.

Imagine how People may Argue Against You

A good way of persuading people is to imagine how they would argue against you, and answer their points. Imagine you're writing a letter to persuade the RSPCA to let you work for them...

First think up all the arguments against your opinion.

Reasons they wouldn't accept me

- too young
- not enough time to spend
- lack of experience
- what could I actually do to help?

Then you've got to work out how to prove them wrong.

- too young — but parents say it's OK
- lack of experience — but want to learn & love animals
- no time — can arrange to do it at weekends & after school
- what could I do? — willing to do anything to help

Me? Automatically disagree? Absolutely not...

REMEMBER — think like your reader and you'll always be one step ahead of them. Which means you'll be able to persuade them you're right... AHA HA HA... AHA HA HA... *[evil laughter]*

Persuasive Writing Tools

Writing a really persuasive argument can be hard work — here are some more tips to help you out.

Keep your writing Polite

1) Being polite is important when you're writing about people with the opposite opinion to yours.
2) You should criticise their opinions only — don't criticise them personally, or you'll sound angry.

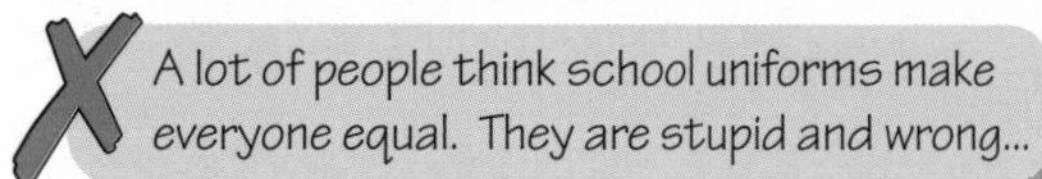

A lot of people think school uniforms make everyone equal. They are stupid and wrong...

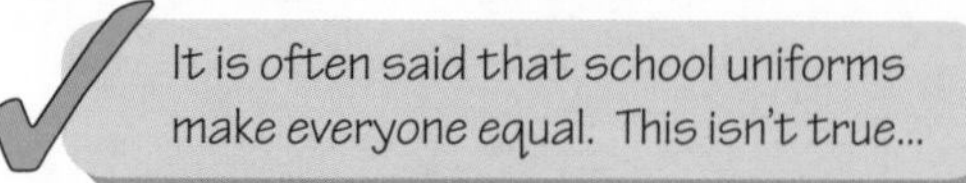

It is often said that school uniforms make everyone equal. This isn't true...

Talk Directly to your readers

You can use "you" to talk directly to your readers, especially if you're trying to persuade them to do something.

Giving blood saves lives. As a caring person, do you really need to read further before you take action?

Stories from Real Life can be Entertaining

1) Stories from real life can be a great way to persuade people by entertaining them — but keep them short.
2) You can make them up too, as long as they're realistic.

Say you want to persuade parents to let their children cycle to school. Telling a funny story about when you were stuck in a really terrible traffic jam could persuade parents not to drive their kids to school.

Stories can also be more serious. E.g. if you're persuading a local MP that the pavements in your street are dangerous, you could write about a time when your granny tripped and fell.

Our Dave was strangled by his stupid school tie...

Fantastic — three ways of making your writing as punchy as a boxing octopus. Use them wisely and they'll help get the audience on your side, and help them understand the points you're making.

Writing to Inform, Explain or Advise

Non-fiction writing can inform, explain or advise — make sure you know what each one means.

Pick out the Key Words in the question

You need a clear idea of your purpose and your audience.
Key words in the question will tell you what the question's asking:

> Q1. You are planning to open a shop in the town where you live.
> Write the text for a leaflet informing local residents about the shop.
> The leaflet should be about:
> - where the shop will be
> - what the shop will sell
> - who the shop is for

Informing is about Giving Information to your reader

Writing to inform means telling your readers about a topic they may not know much about.

1) Informative writing can be practical — e.g. a government leaflet giving information about Swine Flu.
2) Sometimes it can be more personal — e.g. a writer informing readers about the time they ran the marathon.

In either case, you should include plenty of clear facts.

Explaining means helping your readers Understand

When you're explaining, you need to assume your readers don't understand the subject.

1) You need to give facts, examples and evidence.
2) First decide on the main points you want to make.
   Then make sure each point is explained with an example or fact.
3) It's also important to tell your readers what any technical terms you use mean — see page 29.

Advice needs to be based on the Facts

You might have to advise your readers, e.g. a letter to the council suggesting improvements to a sports centre.

1) Advice should follow on from information you've already written.
2) Keep your advice formal and positive. Don't write things like, "It's obvious that this should have been done years ago".

"Perhaps the swimming pool could be extended..."

Advice about advice? Too much information...

Informing and explaining involve telling your readers what they need to know. If you're giving out advice, make sure it's based on what you've told them. Oh, and never mix milk with orange juice.

Writing to Inform, Explain or Advise

Here's some more helpful advice about writing to inform, explain or advise.

Plan your writing carefully

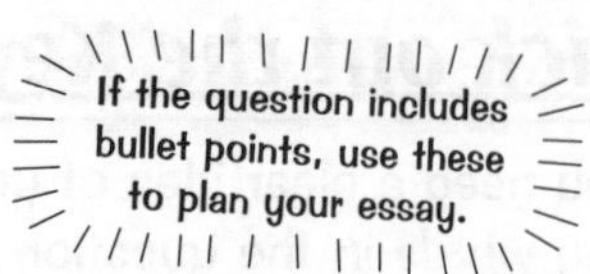

If the question includes bullet points, use these to plan your essay.

Think about the main things you want to say and note them down in a plan.
Here's an example of a "writing to inform" question.

> Write the text for an information leaflet about the sixth form at your school for potential students and their parents.

And here's a plan of the main points you might want to mention in your answer.

Purpose: to inform
Form: leaflet
Audience: potential students and their parents.
Points to include:
1) Big school — 1500 pupils.
2) There's loads of choice of subjects.
3) Students get good grades.

Layout can help you Organise your writing

If you're writing a leaflet, you can use headings and bullet points to organise the text:

1) Headings break text up into sections and tell the reader what that section is about.
2) Bullet points are a good way to split information into lists of facts.

Using "I" or "You" can sound too personal

If you use "I..." a lot, it can sound as if you're just expressing your opinion.
That's fine for some pieces but it can make information or advice sound unconvincing.

Don't say:

I have noticed that the temperature of the swimming pool water has been rising for the last 3 months.

This leaves room for doubt — did you just 'notice', or did you actually measure it?

Say:

The temperature of the swimming pool water has been rising over the last 3 months.

Sounds like a statement of fact.

Use silver bullet points if you're writing about werewolves...

Using headings and bullet points can help to give your writing a really clear structure, but you should only use them if they're suitable for the form you've been asked to write in.

Make Sure Everyone Can Understand

You've got to make sure that everyone knows what you're on about.

Think about your Readers

If you're writing to inform or explain, don't assume your will readers know everything about the topic.

1) Explain things which might be obvious to you, but not necessarily obvious to other people.

This is no good —

Get a plant and grow it.

You need to explain what you mean —

Buy some seeds from a garden centre. Dig a small hole and put the seeds in the hole. Water the area regularly.

2) Try to guess where the reader might get confused and make those bits especially clear.

Explain Technical terms...

1) Your writing should be clear enough for anyone to understand.
2) Take care even when you're explaining something as ordinary as cooking dinner — some readers still might not understand the technical terms you're using.

The underlined words here are technical terms. They'll be understood by tennis fans...

The serve-volley game of Williams dominated Davenport's ground strokes. She repeatedly got to the net allowing her to take the first set.

...but others may not understand, and get confused.

...but don't make your language Too Simple

1) If you don't use the right words, it might seem like you don't know what you're talking about....

There are several different types of singer. Some singers sound really squeaky when they sing, and some singers don't.

This is all pretty obvious — it would be better if the writer had named and explained the different types of voice (soprano, baritone etc.).

2) ... and sometimes it might be unclear what you mean.

I have spoken to many people and many of them are concerned about graffiti in the local area.

'Many' is vague — be more specific and explain how many people and who they are (students, parents etc.).

But it all made perfect sense to me...

Burble, jabber, wibber, phtang... See how that technical jargon got you all confused — well, it's the same in the exam. Explain the tricky stuff properly, and you'll get more lovely, lovely marks.

Useful Language for Non-Fiction Texts

Want your non-fiction writing to sparkle like a diamond in an exploding tinsel factory? Read on...

Use Rhetorical Questions to Involve your audience

1) A rhetorical question doesn't need an answer — the answer should be obvious from the text.

Is this sort of thing acceptable in our society?

2) Leaving the readers to put the answer together themselves is a great way of making them agree with you.

Use emotional language (like "ruining the countryside") to emphasise your feelings on the subject.

Can anyone tell me why road builders are ruining the countryside?

Use Lists of Threes

It's one of the easiest and most useful tricks for emphasising your points.
Instead of just using one adjective in a sentence, use three.

Making children sit more exams would be stressful, time-consuming and unreasonable.

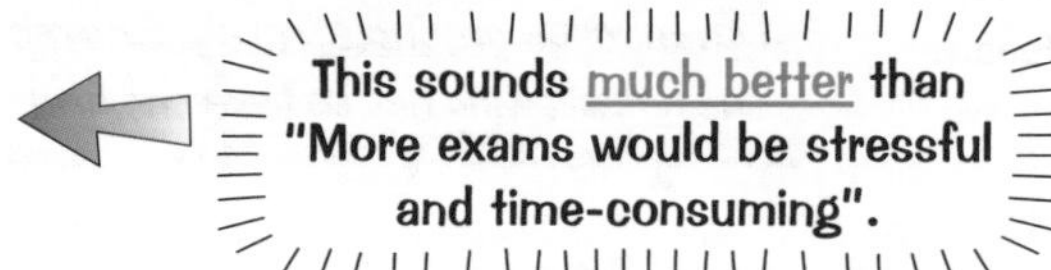

This sounds much better than "More exams would be stressful and time-consuming".

Be Careful when you're using Exaggeration

1) Sometimes you can use an exaggeration in your writing to make your point sound stronger.

These days, teachers have to wade through tonnes of paperwork every week.

Your readers will realise you don't literally mean tonnes. It just stresses that you're talking about a lot of paperwork.

2) Use exaggeration carefully. If it's not obvious to the reader that you're exaggerating, they might think you're just a bit confused.

This exaggeration is the best thing ever!

The techniques on this page can be very powerful. But like a powerful, er, firework (bear with me), they could go off in your face. Use them with care, or you may give your readers the wrong message.

Revision Summary

This section has covered the main forms of non-fiction texts you're likely to come across during your English course, but don't panic if you get something a bit different — the basic advice is still the same. Think about your readers and what you're trying to achieve. Just to make sure you've got the hang of it, here's a page load of questions to test your knowledge.

1) How should your style of writing be different in a formal and an informal letter?
2) Name two techniques you could use in a newspaper article to make it easier to read.
3) If you're writing a film review, why is it important to include some facts about the film itself?
4) What's the main difference between a speech and other types of non-fiction text?
5) Give three examples of audiences you might write for. Say whether you would write in a formal or informal way for each one.
6) Put these points of a plan for a persuasive answer into the correct order:
Emotional argument, Introduction, Logical argument, Conclusion, Other points of view.
7) Why is it important to be logical in your thinking?
8) How can using emotion help your argument?
9) Why might the sentence "Everyone has the right to an education" help get the reader on your side?
10) Why is it important to support your argument with facts?
11) Which of these quotes would be appropriate in an essay on getting good grades, and why?
    a) "Exams changed my entire existence", said a stranger in the street.
    b) "Getting good GCSEs has helped me to achieve what I want in life", said Simon von Norbury, Head of Marketing, Beards and Brogues Ltd.
12) Do all the facts and opinions you use in non-fiction answers have to come from real sources?
13) Do you need to try to put yourself in the reader's shoes? Why?
14) Why should you address any concerns you think your reader might have about your argument?
15) Give one reason why you might include a story from real life in your writing.
16) What's the main difference between informing readers about something and explaining it to them?
17) Why should you explain any technical terms you use in your writing?
18) What is a rhetorical question and why are rhetorical questions effective?

Different Types of Creative Writing

These pages cover types of creative writing — check with your teacher which ones you're doing.

Scripts and Speeches are Spoken

This stuff will also come in useful for the 'Writing for the Spoken Voice' part of Edexcel English Language.

1) Text for a script or speech (see p.34) can be written in the voice of a specific person, e.g. a character from a piece of fiction.
2) You'll usually be told who your audience is and/or what the theme is.
3) Think about what kind of words characters would use, whether they use formal language or a dialect.
4) If your script is for more than one person, give each person their own style.

Articles and Reviews can Entertain

1) You'll usually be told what kind of audience or publication you're writing for. For example, it could be a film review for a website aimed at teenagers.
2) Think about purpose of the text, e.g.:

- an article in a magazine could be either humorous or serious.
- a film review should give an opinion — it shouldn't just describe what happens in the film.
- a news article will be serious in style, but could include quotes and descriptions.

Descriptive Writing and Stories also Entertain

1) You might have to tell a story or describe a scene (see p.37-40).
2) You may be given the title or maybe the first or last sentence .
3) You might be asked to write from your own point of view, or from someone else's point of view.

Voice-overs explain Images

1) Voice-overs are the scripts that go with documentaries, TV adverts, etc (see p.34). They can be informative, like the example on p.34, or persuasive, like this:

Scene: Slim, happy people playing frisbee on the beach
Voice-over: Would you like to get fit, but don't have the time? Would you like to tone up, but can't afford expensive gym fees? Fallon's home gym could be the answer you're looking for...

2) If you're asked to write a voice-over you need to decide what images it will go with and describe them.

Everyone loves a story — especially about dogs and homework

These are just some examples of creative writing, but there are loads more, e.g. leaflets, emails, blogs... Whatever you're writing, always think about your audience and purpose.

Planning Your Writing

Welcome to Page 33, Planning Your Writing. It really is a smashing little page.

Structure your writing to suit the Purpose

1) Use a structure that suits what you want your writing to achieve.
2) You won't get any marks for layout, only content.
3) Bear in mind how many words you're expected to write.
4) Make it really clear which bits are important. Add details and vary your style.
5) Write out a detailed plan.

My writing always suits my porpoise.

For example, if you're planning a short story:

- Start with something unusual or exciting that will make your reader curious.
- As long as you have a plot worked out, you can use any order you like.
- Just be sure to keep it relevant. Make sure that every point is related to the story.

You could have a character running from something — this'll get your reader wondering why.

Your character could be very old at the start of the story, then they could talk about events that happened when they were young.

Choose your writing Style to match your Audience

Work out who your audience is before you start writing, and think about what style you need to use:

Write a report for a local newspaper on the discovery of the bodies of Romeo and Juliet.

Keep the tone of your writing formal. Readers wouldn't expect a funny report about death.

If you're writing for a teenage audience, you can be more informal.

You've been asked to write film review for a website aimed at teenagers.

If you're not told who the audience is, just write for the examiner and keep it fairly formal.

Give your readers structure — or they might lose the plot...

Your readers will notice if your writing doesn't make sense or has irrelevant bits. Emphasise important points by going into detail and using different styles.

Moving Images

Moving what? What I mean is 'Here's a great chance to write about movies and TV shows'.

You might have to Write a Film Review

1) **Provide information about the film — e.g. what it's about.**
2) **Think about who you're writing for and whether they'd enjoy the film.**
3) **Persuasive language is useful if you're trying to convince people to see it.**

> This sci-fi summer blockbuster is packed full of amazing CGI. Galaxies explode, new worlds are discovered and alien forces fight.

List of three used to build excitement.

Specialist words related to films.

You could be writing a Script or a Voice-over

Voice-overs are read out by an unseen presenter to tell the viewer about the images on screen, e.g. in adverts and documentaries.

> Scene: Underwater, daytime, blind fish swimming
> Voice-over: Isolated for generations in a network of caves beneath the Rio Grande, the Mexican Tetra has developed several unique adaptations to life in a world without light. These creatures have no eyes and each one is pinkish-white...

Show what viewers would see.

Give lots of information.

Give the voice-over person plenty of chances to take a breath.

You could write a Short Story for a Film to be Based On

You might have to write a text that will be adapted for a film or TV drama. These texts need to have detailed descriptions to tell the director how you imagine the characters and settings.

> Late one misty Bristol evening in autumn 1879, Dr Procktar headed to the quayside. As always, he wore his trademark battered brown overcoat. The frayed bullet hole in the left lapel was now a vivid reminder of how fortunate he had been in Munich, just two months earlier...

This gives loads of detail that the director could use.

Describe the lead character to give the director clues.

Sets up a possible flashback and suggests more settings.

Alice in Wonderland — based on a true story...

If a picture says a thousand words and a film is shot at 24 frames a second and lasts 162 minutes — I make that two-hundred and thirty three million, two hundred and eighty thousand words. Whoa.

Re-creations

You can turn fiction texts into different types of writing. Cool, eh?

You might change a Play or Poem into a Short Story...

1) Turning something into a short story gives you the chance to add to the original text.
2) You could use the speech, characters and stage directions from plays, or the feelings and themes from a poem.
3) You could change it so it's written from the point of view of one of the characters.
4) Here's an example of how you could change a scene from Macbeth into a short story:

You could use actual lines from the play or change them.

Extra details add excitement.

"Why did you bring these daggers from the place?" hissed Lady Macbeth, glaring at the sight of her husband's crimson hands, and making no effort to hide her impatience with him. Macbeth's vacant gaze drifted from her stern brow to the weapon trembling in his palm as though trying to free itself from his twisted fingers...

...or change a Text into Non-Fiction Prose...

1) Non-fiction prose could mean things like articles or radio broadcasts.
2) For example the events in 'Of Mice and Men' could be turned into a newspaper article:

The headline is appropriate for an article.

Details show you understand the original text.

LOCAL MAN AND WOMAN FOUND DEAD
Details are emerging, after two bodies were found near Soledad yesterday. The first, the body of a young female, was found in a barn in the late afternoon. Less than an hour after the discovery of the woman, a second fatality was reported in an area of woodland just three quarters of a mile away. It is understood that the deaths are both being treated as suspicious, and are believed to be linked in some way.

Crime reports usually include factual detail.

These phrases make it sound more formal.

Adapt the text to a script for 'George and Lennie On Ice'...

There are lots of different options for this task. For example, you might be asked to change a website into a blog, or an image into a film script, or a radio podcast into a diary entry.

Commissions

Having to write on a specific theme is a bit daunting — that's why planning is the key to success.

Some Themes have lots of *Different Meanings*

1) You might be asked to write on a theme that seems pretty vague.
2) It could be something with more than one meaning or a broad topic like this:

> Write a creative piece on the theme 'The Four Seasons'.

3) Scribble down all the things that spring to mind straight away.
4) Once you've jotted down all you can, decide which idea to write about.
5) Then think about the purpose of your text, what form it'll take and who you're writing it for.

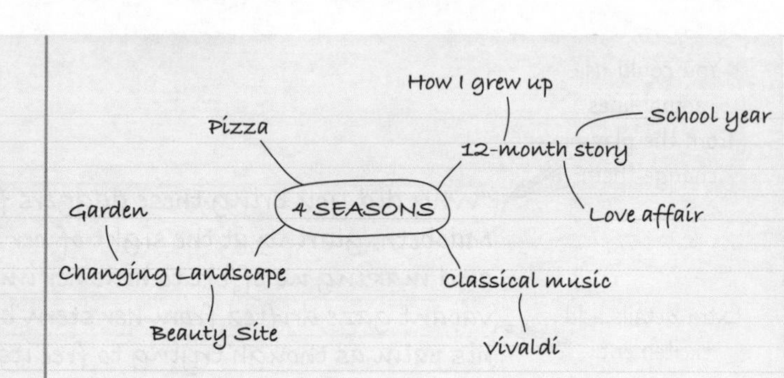

Other Themes can be more *Specific*

1) You might choose a task where you have to do a particular type of creative writing.
2) The purpose, form or audience may have already been decided for you.
3) Have a look at the questions below for an idea of the kinds of things you might get:

> Write a letter to the town council explaining a problem in the town and how it could be solved.

Purpose: inform/advise
Form: letter
Audience: councillors

> Write an article about one of your hobbies for your school or club website.

Purpose: inform (& persuade?)
Form: online article with lots of facts
Audience: school community / visitors

It's easier than writing about Ham and Pineapple...

Be smart. Pick a topic to suit your strengths and style — if possible, write about things you're interested in. And remember, if you want to get plenty of marks it helps to plan your answers.

Descriptive Writing

This is essential for creative writing, but you'll also need to write descriptively for writing non-fiction.

You're painting a Picture with Words

1) When you're writing to describe, remember that the reader won't have the same picture in their head as you have in yours — you need to draw it for them with words.
2) Come up with creative ways to describe what you're thinking about.
3) You can use your own experiences — but remember you can add in invented details too.

Imagine you're making a Film of the scene

Imagine that you're making a film of your scene, and you're describing what will happen in it.

1) Think about how the scene will look at different times of the day, or in different seasons.

> The beach was lonely and grey, empty of all movement except the soft splash of waves. It was hard to believe that it would soon be alive with tourists and brightly-coloured deck chairs.

2) Or you could zoom in or out of your scene, describing things as you go.

> I was only feet away from the last of the day's fishermen looking out to sea. The reflections of trees shimmered on the water, and in the distance I could just make out the hazy form of hills.

Think about each of the Senses when you write

You can't use every single one all the time but the senses can be used to make a scene come to life.

The wall crumbled away to reveal a small tunnel winding into the distance.

Sam heard a faint, dripping sound from inside the cave.

As she walked on, a smell like rotting vegetables filled her nostrils.

The soup tasted salty and contained lots of chewy lumps.

There was a sharp crunch under her foot. It felt like the shell of a snail cracking.

Oh daarling, I'm simply overcome with all this loveliness...

OK so all this "paint a picture with words" stuff might sound weird, but it's the best way to get this right. Make sure you use a broad range of language and describe things using different senses.

Narrative Writing

Narrative writing is a chance to write a story. You might be given a title or a sentence to use, but it's pretty much up to you what you write about — so choose something that you're interested in.

Get your story straight Before you start writing

Once you've got a rough idea of the plot, write a brief synopsis of your story — a breakdown of the plot.

1) Beginning — Start by introducing your key characters.

A lot of stories are about conflict or a struggle. That's because characters have different motives which clash.

2) Build-up — What's going to happen — how will you build up to the climax of your story?

Give your characters a challenge. There has to be an element of risk to make it exciting.

3) Climax — The main event or turning point should happen now.

You need to build up the suspense and keep your reader guessing up until this point.

4) Ending — Be sure that your conclusion makes some kind of point.

You could give the story a moral, or end it with an unexpected twist.

Check that your story has These Things

1) An entertaining plot that says something.
2) A clear structure with a beginning, middle and end.
3) Different sentence structures and interesting vocabulary.
4) Realistic and entertaining dialogue.
5) Whatever was stated in the question, e.g. the first line.
6) Correct paragraphs, punctuation and spelling.

Honestly, Officer, this is a crucial part of an entertaining plot...

My story's all wonky — there's a twist in the tail...

Once you've got a brilliant idea for a plot, you can turn it into a heart-stoppingly good story by really thinking about the structure of your writing. Keep the four plot stages in your mind.

Narrative Writing

Bring characters to life and make things more interesting by including lots of detail and emotions.

Write good Descriptions using Images

1) Give specific details that set the scene for the reader, and help emphasise the important points.
2) Use inventive images to get the reader to create a mental picture of what's happening.

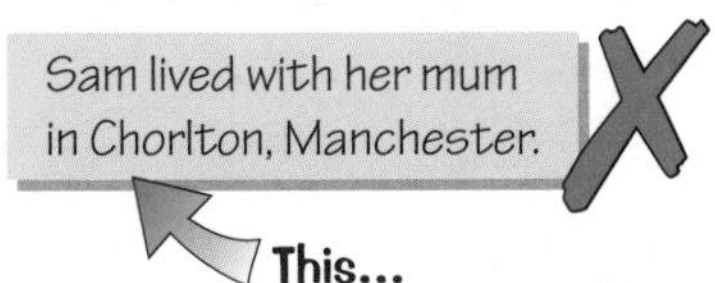

Sam lived with her mum
in Chorlton, Manchester.

Sam lived in Chorlton, Manchester with her mum. She spent most of her time in her tiny attic bedroom. It was a damp, musty place, and she often heard rats scuttling at night.

This... ...is not as good as this.

Write from your Own Viewpoint or from Someone Else's...

1) A good story gets inside the characters' heads and really thinks about their thoughts and feelings.
2) One way of doing this is to write from your own viewpoint — e.g. you could write a story about something that happened to you (see p.26). For example:

> I've always loved horse-riding, the thrill of the gallop, the sweet smell of hoof-crushed grass, the unspoken understanding as my horse and I move as one. But the bond between me and my horse, Cloud, was really tested one windswept evening in November.

3) Another good way of getting inside a character's head is to write down the thoughts the character is having, as if they were speaking them out loud. For example:

> Emily stood by her window, getting ready to lower a basket of treats from her bedroom to children in the street below. "I must remember not to lean out too far," she thought to herself. "I don't want strangers to see me."

4) You need to really think about why you (or the character) feel the way you do — e.g. don't just start a story with "Erin was scared of dogs", explain why she was scared.

Make the Important parts really Stand Out

You have to make sure your reader really understands which bits are important. Give details and try to vary your style and vocabulary.

Think about why what you're describing matters:

1) Who cares about it?
2) What effect does it have on your characters?
3) How does it influence what happens in the plot?

Bring feelings into it — you know it makes sense...

"Mrs Chalice was looking so lovely," he thought to himself, "but she could never like me, could she? Where am I? Day-dreaming again. Oh, and I was going to write about bringing stories to life. Oops."

Style and Finishing Your Narrative

Your writing will work better if you don't always write in exactly the same way.

Vary your Structure and Style

Changing the pace and style of your sentences and paragraphs will make your writing more interesting. You could change between long, descriptive sentences and shorter ones to match the mood of your story.

These sentences are short. They sound slower.

> *It was Ahab's turn to keep watch. All his shipmates were gently nodding off to sleep. Even the waves seemed to nod slowly as if in a trance. Out of nowhere a gigantic whale surfaced right by the boat, blowing out a thousand bubbles, and everyone woke up and shouted, clutching at the rails for safety.*

This sentence is longer. It speeds up, and sounds more energetic.

Short sentences don't always slow the pace down. They can be short and punchy to describe action scenes.

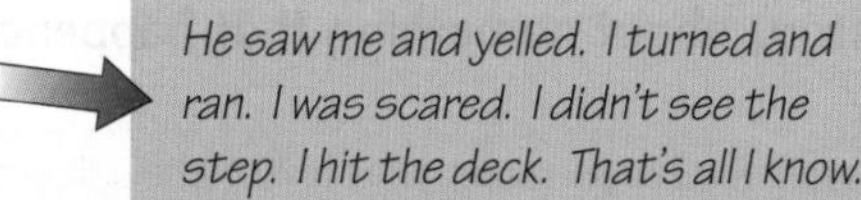
He saw me and yelled. I turned and ran. I was scared. I didn't see the step. I hit the deck. That's all I know.

Plan the Ending carefully

It's worth spending a bit of time planning the conclusion (see p.38).

A twist
in the tail? Oh my,
this is dreadful
news...

1) You could aim for the unexpected by finishing your story with a twist. Drop some hints earlier on in the plot, to refer back to.
2) Give your plot a moral so that the story proves a point. You could borrow a moral from a fairy tale.
3) You need a paragraph at the end of your story that ties up all the loose ends of the plot.
4) The very last line is important — it needs to be written clearly and cleverly, so that it sums up the story for the reader and leaves them satisfied.

Pace yourself Ahab — we've a little whale to go yet...

It's vital to vary the pace in your story to keep the reader interested — then they'll want to read all the way to the end. Don't ever, ever disappoint them and finish by saying it was all a dream.

Getting Through the Assessment

You can't just wing a controlled assessment with no preparation. N.B. Depending on your specification, you might have to do some creative writing in an exam as well.

Double Check exactly what you have to do

You'll have to do at least one creative writing task as part of the controlled assessment.

1) Check that you know how many tasks you have to do.
2) Know how long you have to complete each task and how many words you'll have to write. If there isn't a word limit, you'll be given some guidance on roughly how much to write.
3) Read the instructions carefully.

Do your Research and Preparation Carefully

1) Use your preparation time to work out the key points to include.
2) You can use the internet, books and other resources for your research.
3) When you're doing research, make loads of notes. Always write down where you got information from so you'll be able to find it again quickly.
4) When you've completed your research write up neat copies of your notes to take into the assessment. You can't take a draft answer in with you but you can take in a short plan so make it neat, clear and useful.

I said a short plan, Norman.

Check Your Grammar and Presentation at the end

1) Leave yourself enough time at the end of each task to read through it carefully.

- Check that your writing is clear and readable.
- Check your spelling. You won't have access to dictionaries or spell-checkers so double-check any difficult words.
- Check your punctuation and grammar.

2) When the time's up make sure you've filled in your candidate details before you hand it in.

Plan your way to a great assessment — then plan to celebrate...

And that's it — how to have a happy controlled assessment.

Revision Summary

Loads of people get really worried over this original writing bit — but you just need to learn the tricks that make stories seem really interesting and clever.

So make sure you go through every single one of these questions and examples, and you'll see just how easy it can be.

1) What is a voice-over?
2) If you're not told who your audience is, what kind of style should you write in?
3) Why do you need to include plenty of pauses when writing scripts and voice-overs?
4) If you're writing a text that will be adapted for the screen, how can you help the director?
5) You have been commissioned to write creative pieces for the following themes. Jot down three ideas for:
   a) Hair
   b) Escape
   c) Moving Out
6) a) Write a <u>good</u> and a <u>bad</u> description of someone's face (a few sentences is fine).
   b) Explain why one is better than the other.
7) Why might it be helpful to write about your own experiences?
8) Choose two of the five senses and give an example of how each might be used to describe a house in a short story.
9) For each of the following parts of a story, explain what each one should do:
   a) Beginning
   b) Build-up
   c) Climax
   d) Ending
10) True or false: You shouldn't think about a character's thoughts and feelings when writing a story?
11) Let's say you've just had a trip on a magic flying carpet. Write an interesting paragraph about your trip (tips on p.39-40).
12) What could you do to make sure your creative writing has a strong ending?
13) What kind of notes can you take in to your controlled assessment?
14) What should you check for once you've finished writing?

Writing About Prose, Drama and Poetry

There are different types of literature questions and you need to know how to answer all of them.

What you have to Study

1) You'll definitely have to answer a question on Shakespeare and one on a text from a different culture.
2) You'll probably have to answer a question on a 'literary heritage' text.
3) You might also have to write about another play, some poetry or a prose text, like a novel or short story.

Now here's how to tackle literature questions...

Step 1 — work out What The Question Is About

1) The question's likely to be about one of four things:

- **THEME** — what the play, poem or story is about, e.g. love/conflict.
- **SETTING** — the importance of the place(s) where the text is set.
- **CHARACTERISATION** — how the writer puts across information about the characters.
- **WRITER'S SKILLS** — the techniques that the writer uses to influence the reader.

2) When you're writing about a text from a different culture or from the literary heritage you'll also have to write about the time period and culture the text was written in, and how it links with the text (see p.49).

Step 2 — Break the question into Bullet Points

We've just used 'Little Red Riding Hood' as an example in this book — you won't actually get questions on it.

1) You can't just give a one-sentence answer to literature questions. You have to go into detail and make lots of separate points.

> Write about the ways in which Little Red Riding Hood is shown to change or stay the same in the course of the story.

2) The exam paper might help you by breaking the question down into bullets. If it doesn't, try to come up with some of your own.

> Write about:
> - what she says and does
> - her attitudes and feelings
> - how the writer shows you how she changes or stays the same.

Figure out the first two things and it'll help you work out the answer.

Choose wisely you must...

If you get a choice of questions, it'd make sense to pick one which gives you lots of ideas of stuff to write. Make sure you're answering on a text you've actually studied too...

Writing About Prose, Drama and Poetry

Now you've really got to grips with the question, follow these steps to write a great answer.

Step 3 — now make a Plan

Write a plan based on your own bullet points or the ones you've been given.

- BEGINNING - picking flowers, no hurry to get to Grandma's; END - she tricks wolf
- BEGINNING - feels confident and secure; END - cross with herself, even more confident
- BEGINNING - "drifted along", compares her to butterfly; END - looks the wolf in the eye, "now she knew what to do"

Choose things that show how she changes.

Step 4 — write a brief Introduction then follow the plan

Your introduction should be pretty short — just like a quick answer to the question.

> There are several events in the story which show how Little Red Riding Hood changes — such as the escape from Grandmother's house. They show how she starts off trusting, but learns from her experience.

The rest of your essay should back up what you say in the introduction.

1) Deal with the bullet points in order.
2) Don't chop and change between different ideas. Deal with one idea at a time in separate paragraphs.

Can you help me cross the road dear?
I'm not falling for that old trick grandma.

Step 5 — Talk about your Personal Response

1) You need to talk about your personal response to the text — what you think the author's trying to say and how they're trying to make the reader feel.
2) There are lots of different ways of interpreting a text — use quotes to back up your interpretation.
3) Your response needs to fit the question. If it's 'How does the writer present the character of Little Red Riding Hood?' say 'The reader feels surprised that such an innocent young girl manages to outsmart the wolf in the end.'

Step 6 — don't forget the Conclusion

Make sure you've answered the question. Sum up by stating your main idea again — but in different words.

> At the start of the story Little Red Riding Hood doesn't have a care in the world. By the end she has been through a terrifying experience. The writer shows that she has learnt from her experience and become more cautious.

'Mine are lacy, but they've gone a bit grey' — A briefs introduction...

If there's not enough in your plan, there won't be enough in your essay. Simple as that. Get the planning right and not only will the essay be easier to write, it'll be a better essay.

Writing About Characters

You might need to talk about the way the author <u>creates</u> their characters.

Characters are always there for a Reason

1) When you're answering a question about a character in a poem, play or novel, don't talk about them as if they're real people — make it clear that the author has <u>created</u> them to help get a message across.
2) A character's <u>appearance</u>, <u>actions</u> and <u>language</u> all help to get this message across.
3) Find descriptions of how they <u>look</u> or what they <u>do</u>, then think about what this might say about them.

LORD OF THE FLIES — WILLIAM GOLDING

Golding's description of Jack's face as "crumpled" and "ugly without silliness" makes us think that he might be an unpleasant person.

OF MICE AND MEN — JOHN STEINBECK

The description of Lennie hurting the puppies when he strokes them tells the reader that he isn't in control of his own strength.

Work out the reasons Why Characters Do Things

1) Some characters are motivated by stuff like...

   Pity, Fear, Money, Love, Power, Greed, Food (well, sometimes), Anger

2) Some characters want things so badly that they <u>use</u> other people.
3) Some characters want to be <u>liked</u>, others want <u>revenge</u> or to feel <u>powerful</u>.

Look at the way characters Speak

1) The way characters, including the narrator, <u>speak</u> tells you a lot about them.
2) The author makes them speak the way they do to get you to see them in a <u>particular way</u>.

"Oh, you're one of those little men who reads the gas meters? How hilarious..."

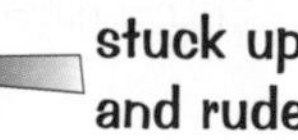

stuck up and rude

"If it's be alright, I mean if you didn't mind, if you could... pass the salt please, Dad?"

painfully shy

In the beginning, there was George, Lennie, a snake and an apple...

Think of the author as being a bit like <u>God</u> — they've made the characters exactly how they want them to be. If only George and Lennie hadn't eaten the beans from the can of knowledge...

Writing About Characters

This stuff should be going through your head whenever you've got a question about a character.

Look at how the characters Treat Other People

The writer can tell you a lot about their characters by showing you how they get on with others. It can reveal sides to their character that they keep hidden from the other main characters.

> Everyone loved Jack and thought he was warm and caring. But when a homeless man shuffled up and asked him for change, Jack spat into the man's face, saying "Don't ever speak to me again old man, or you'll be sorry."

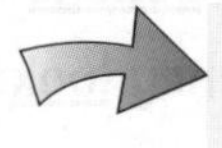

> Although people believe Jack is warm and caring, he is actually rude and mean.

Stories can Tell You what characters Think

1) Novels and short stories give descriptions of characters' thoughts and behaviour — the voice telling the story fills you in on what characters are thinking.
2) Pinpoint those bits, quote them, and say how they help answer the question.

> Sarah was disgusted by Jamie's behaviour at the bar and refused to speak to him.

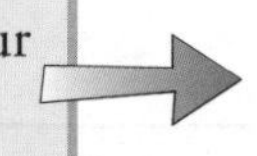

> Sarah's reaction might make the reader think about Jamie in the same way.

3) Books with a third-person narrator (who isn't one of the characters), let you in on the secret thoughts of all the characters.

> Tamasine didn't want to tell anyone that she was ill.

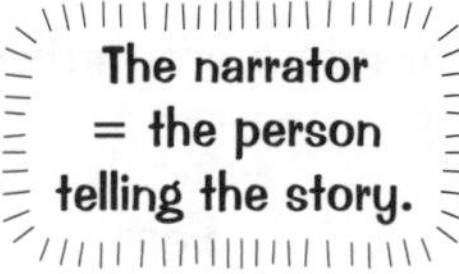

The story can be Told by one of the Characters

When the story is told by one of the characters it's called first-person narration.

1) First person narration gives you a first hand description of what the character sees, says, and thinks.
2) Find bits where they tell you what they're like, or give away what they're like by their attitudes.

> All the other people there were boring fools. No one had anything interesting to say to me.

> The narrator feels that he is better than the other guests. He sounds very arrogant.

3) First person narrators can't always be trusted because you're only getting one side of the story.

First person narrators — would you Adam an' Eve it?

Remember that the narrator has been created in a particular way by the author — think about why. Also, don't forget that first-person narrators only give one side of the story.

The Writer's Ideas, Attitudes and Feelings

All authors have **something to say**. All you need to do is write about what that is...

Message questions can be hard to spot

1) Questions about the message come in lots of **different forms**:

When the Woodcutter kills the Wolf what is the writer trying to show?

How does the author present ideas about hunger in the novel?

Why do you think the Woodcutter is important?

2) They're all asking the **same** thing:

I'm not bad, I just like dressing up, OK?

What does the writer think? Write about all the bits of the text that give it away.

Work Out the Message of your set texts Before the Exams

Work out the message of a text by making notes on the following things, like I've done for 'Of Mice and Men'.

STORY

George and Lennie are friends who go to work at a ranch but dream of owning their own farm. Lennie keeps doing things wrong and other people don't understand him. This leads to his death.

CHARACTERS

Their relationships with each other cause problems for many of the characters. The happiest characters in the book are the ones like Slim, who avoid close relationships.

TONE

Most characters dream about having a better life, as life on the ranch is sad and lonely.

TITLE

The title refers to a poem by Robert Burns. It means that even the most carefully thought-out plans can go wrong.

Once you've done that, **put it all together** to work out what the message is. I'd say it's something like...

The American Dream of a better, happier life is unrealistic but people still cling to it.

These notes are the **evidence** you need to back up the points you make in your essay.

The writer's message — your dinner's in the oven...

The writer's message could be pretty much anything. Making notes like the ones I've done above for 'Of Mice and Men' is a good way to start figuring out what they might be on about.

The Writer's Techniques

Aha, time for a page all about style. Just think of me as the Gok Wan of literature...

Writing Style affects the way you Feel

The style of a text is a combination of features like these:

words you hear every day	short, simple sentences	lots of fancy comparisons	lots of action
unusual, difficult words	long, complicated sentences	no fancy comparisons	lots of description

Show the examiners you understand how the writer's voice affects you. E.g. If you're saying a character is on the verge of insanity, show how the style backs it up:

The writer makes the character speak in a very confused way.

MAC: I'm late - late - late, better late than never Mother said to me. I'm never late - never been better. So late, so late...

Pay attention to Settings

Writers just love using settings to affect the way you feel about what's happening. You could well get a passage describing a setting from the text, and have to talk about how it's been used to create atmosphere.

> The candlelight cast huge shifting shadows on the mossy walls. The wind howled down the chimney, throwing sparks around the room.
>
> "Dinner is served," the butler announced.

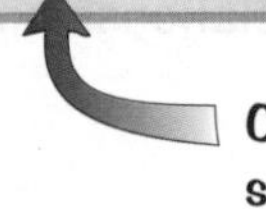

Creepy — could be something awful for dinner.

> The candlelight cast soft shadows around the room. I stretched out lazily in the armchair by the fire.
>
> "Dinner is served," the butler announced.

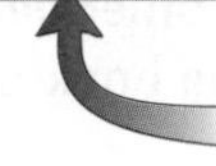

Ah — that sounds a bit more enjoyable.

Look at the Order of Events

1) Stories aren't always told in order. Writers mess around with the order to keep you interested.
2) Flashbacks are where the scene shifts from the present to an event in the past.
3) Foreshadowing is where we're clues about what will happen later in the story.

At the start of Macbeth the Witches predict what will happen to Macbeth.

Everything they predict comes true — though not always in the way Macbeth expects.

Rubber gloves — now they change how you feel...

A writer's individual writing style is called their voice. It affects how the reader feels about characters, ideas and events. If you talk about it in your essay, the examiner will be thrilled.

Different Cultures

"Different Cultures" questions aren't that different from any others. Just look out for these things:

Talk about How the stories are Written

Write about the same stuff as you would in any literature essay, but look out for these things too:

1) Unfamiliar words from other languages or dialects (the words used by people in a certain area).

scuppernong | shinny | drew a bead

2) Words spelt so they sound like an accent or dialect.

purty | fatta the lan' | settin'

Look at the author's Thoughts and Feelings

Think about what the writer wants to say, and write about their values, ideas and attitudes.

1) Feelings about differences between cultures come up all the time.
2) E.g. a text might be about someone who's moved to a different country feeling out of place.
3) Go into detail and be specific.

So don't just say: *She is unhappy because she misses speaking her own language.*

Say: *English is not the poet's mother tongue. Speaking English all the time makes her feel damaged.*

Much better — shows you understand why she's unhappy, and exactly how she feels.

It pays to Know About the writers

I don't see what's so great about the depression.

Try using the Internet to find out a bit about the author you've studied. You won't need to write loads about it, but it might help you come up with some new ideas.

1) Where the writer's from.
2) Information about their experiences.
3) How the poem or story fits in with the writer's life story.

John Steinbeck, Of Mice And Men
1) Born in California in 1902.
2) Spent time working on ranches when he was young.
3) Lived through the Great Depression and saw its effects.

Back in my grandmother's village all the men wore petticoats...

Even if the question asks mainly about the way things are written, don't ignore the thoughts and feelings. The same goes for a thoughts and feelings question — don't ignore the way it's written.

Useful Literature Words

Argh... horrible literature words... Whatever you do, don't panic. Just learn them and you'll be fine.

Try to Use These Words

There's a lot to learn here — but these words are really useful. Learn what they mean and how to spell them.

simile	A simile compares one thing to another. Similes use the words 'like' or 'as'. His socks stank like a dead dog. His dog was as mean as an old PE teacher
metaphor	Metaphors describe one thing as if it were another. Metaphors never use 'like' or 'as'. My car is a heap of old rubbish. My boyfriend is a Greek God.
imagery	This just means using words to build a picture in the reader's mind. Writers often do it by using metaphors and similes.

Don't get these two mixed up. (simile / metaphor)

a symbol	Where an object stands for an emotion or idea. Harry's pigeons flew high above the dismal suburban gardens. If Harry wanted to leave home, the pigeons could be a symbol of freedom.
emotive language	Language that makes you feel a certain way, e.g. sad or angry. Mean-faced Robbie stole the purse from Shelley's kind and cuddly grandma.
personification	When an object, or something in nature, is given human characteristics. The washing line sighed wearily under the weight of the laundry.

ambiguity	Words or events can have more than one possible meaning. If you notice something that could mean two or three different things then say so — it'll get you marks.
irony	This is when the words say one thing, but the writer means something else. Say Carter is awful at football and has played badly in a game. The author writes: Carter really excelled himself this time. He's being ironic — he actually means "Carter played even worse than usual."

I got my boyfriend off a dating site for hotties — Met-a-phwoar...

If you forget one of these words in the exam, don't panic. If you can see a writer's used some clever technique but you're not sure what to call it, then just describe it in your own words.

Comparing

The examples on this page are about poems, but you could be asked to compare any of your texts.

Comparing = finding Similarities and Differences

Comparing means looking at two or more things together, and describing their similarities and differences.

> Compare these two poems. You should consider:
> – the language used
> – the ideas they contain
> – how the poems are presented

Compare both things in Every Paragraph

Write about both texts together — make links between them.
Tackle each point in the question in turn.

– whether the language used in the poems is similar or different

In 'The Charge of the Light Brigade' Tennyson describes war using violent language, such as "Sabring the gunners." In contrast, Owen uses peaceful language like "whispering of fields half-sown" to describe the silence of the battlefield after the fighting.

② – the ideas they contain, and whether they're similar or different.

The soldier in 'Futility' has no name, which shows us that he has lost his individuality in battle. Similarly, in 'The Charge of the Light Brigade' Tennyson refers to the six hundred men as a group, so his soldiers don't have separate identities either.

– how the poems are presented, e.g. whether they are structured in the same way or not.

In 'Futility' both stanzas start with a command, which involves the reader in the poem. In 'Charge of the Light Brigade,' Tennyson involves the reader by using lots of repetition to remind them about how awful the battle was for the soldiers.

I compared her to a summer's day — then she slapped me...

You could also be asked to compare the characters, messages, settings, structure or use of imagery in two texts. Make sure you think about these things before the exam and you're sorted.

Revision Summary

These questions are a darned good measure of what you've taken in and what's dribbled out of your earholes — so make sure you do them.

1) What two kinds of text will you definitely have to answer a question on?
2) 'It's fine to give a one sentence answer to literature questions.' True or false?
3) What must you make sure you cover in your plan?
4) What should you put in the introduction to your answer:
   a) At least eight good points b) The dog's dinner c) A brief answer to the question
5) What does 'personal response' mean?
6) Should you use different words when you sum up your main idea in your conclusion?
7) When you're writing about characters, should you talk about them as if they're real people?
8) Which <u>two</u> of these are <u>not</u> ways in which characters help to get the writer's message across?
   a) The reasons why they do things b) The size of their feet
   c) Standing in the street holding a big sign d) The way they speak
9) Why might an author choose to use a narrator who is not a character in the text?
10) When a text is narrated by one of the characters why can't you trust what they say?
11) Think of one of the texts you've been studying in English lessons.
    Try to sum up the message of the text in one sentence.
12) List any three features of writing style.
13) What do authors usually use settings for?
14) What are flashbacks?
    a) The parts where the scene shifts to an earlier time.
    b) The bits that don't make any sense.
    c) The things they use to put streaks in your hair.
15) What is foreshadowing?
16) Which two of these are things you should write about when answering a question on a text from a different culture?
    a) How the stories are written.
    b) Your Nan's holiday to Majorca.
    c) Everything you know about the culture in the text.
    d) The author's thoughts and feelings.
17) What might it be worth finding out about each of the authors you've studied?
18) Write a short explanation of what each of these technical terms means:
    i) simile ii) metaphor iii) imagery iv) irony
19) You're preparing for the exam. List three things you could compare in texts beforehand.

What You Have To Do

Basically, you need to be able to show that you've understood the play and the way it's been written.

Show you've Understood the play

1) Show that you understand the order everything happens in so you don't make silly errors.
2) You'll also need to show that you're familiar with all the characters, even the minor ones.
3) You need to quote little bits of text to back up your points and prove you've understood the play.

You've also got to know stuff about the characters — who's related to whom, what are they like, how they behave, etc...

Explain the Major Issues the play deals with

Plays are about more than just the plot. Look out for these things in any play:

1. Social Issues — 'An Inspector Calls' deals with the problems between social classes.
2. Moral Issues — 'The Crucible' deals with justice.

Show you understand the Significance of the play

Almost all plays have something to say about society and beliefs at the time they were written. These are the kinds of themes the writer might touch on:

WAR
What's the point?
Is it a good thing?

JUSTICE
What makes a good ruler?
Can a ruler be fair?

ORDER
Is freedom more important than law and order?

LOVE
What is love?
Is it always a good thing?

FATE
Do we control our own lives?

Come up with some Ideas of your own

1) Teachers and examiners love it if you can come up with something original.
2) As long as you can back it up with a quote from the text, you're sorted.
3) Try to talk about your personal response as well — what effect the text has had on you (e.g. did it make you laugh, cry, sneeze etc.?).

Stop playing around — and get this learnt...

Remember that plays are meant to be acted, not read in your head. So if you're struggling, put on your best thespian's voice and read it aloud — that way the characters will be clearer.

What You Have To Do

When an author writes a play, they'll be thinking about the effect it will have, so you should too.

Write about the Style

1) Say what effects the playwright creates, e.g. suspense, humour, anger...
2) Mention any imagery — see page 50.
3) Try to spot how the words affect the rhythm.
   Short sentences can make a character sound excited.
   Longer sentences slow down the pace of the speech.
4) Look out for repetition — anything that's repeated is important.

'Friends' repeats — so important they even show them in heaven

Show you know that plays should be Watched not Read

You need to show that you realise plays are meant to be performed, so think about the impact a play would have on an audience.

You can do this by throwing in the odd line a bit like this —

> This would look particularly spectacular when performed on stage because of the...

> This is a visual joke that an audience would find very amusing because...

Show you understand Stagecraft

'Stagecraft' means the writer's skill at writing for the stage. Ask yourself:

1. How would this scene look on stage?
2. How would the audience react?
3. Is it effective?

Play scripts are written to be acted out on a stage. So writers use things like silences, actions and sound effects to set a mood or to give the audience information. These are a part of stagecraft too. These things are often mentioned in stage directions (see page 55). Look out for them when you're writing about a scene, and say what effect you think they would have on the audience.

Stagecraft? — I think it's quite similar to knitting...

Crafty lot these playwrights. Another thing they like to do is use different speaking styles for different characters to show their personalities. If you notice that, stick it in your answer for some lovely marks.

Reading Plays

You need to know how plays are different from books and poems to write about them properly.

Plays can be Serious or Funny

Tragedy

1) Tragedy is about big topics — e.g. religion, love, death, war. It usually involves the downfall of the main character.
2) Tragedies are really serious and moving. They often have a moral message.

Comedy

1) Comedies are supposed to make you laugh.
2) Events and characters are based on things that happen in real life, but are much more silly and exaggerated.

Don't forget History Plays — they're any kind of play based on real historical events.

Dialogue is one character talking to Another

1) If two or more people talk to each other it's called dialogue.
2) If one person speaks for a long time (to the audience and/or other characters) it's called a monologue.

LORD CRUMB: Where exactly is the pizza?
VERNON: In the basement, my lord.
LORD CRUMB: Very good, Vernon.

A Soliloquy is thinking Out Loud

A soliloquy is when a character speaks out loud about their thoughts. Only the audience can hear what they're saying — other characters can't hear a thing.

Stage Directions describe the action on stage

You can write about stage directions — they tell you a lot about how the playwright wanted the play to look.

STAGE DESIGNS
scenery, lighting, special effects

A cluttered attic room: stuffed bear, upright piano, pot plants. Moonlight filters through a dirty window.

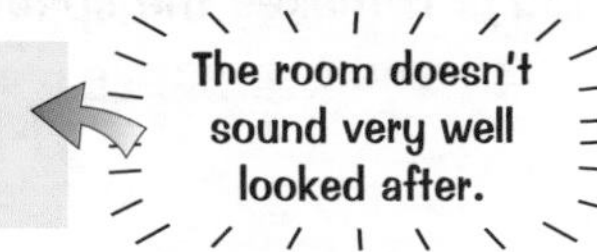

The room doesn't sound very well looked after.

ACTION

Unseen by Lord Crumb, Vernon slides the pizza into an envelope and conceals it beneath a cushion.

I used to talk to myself — but my parents disapproved...

If you ask me, soliloquy is a ridiculous sort of a word. It's not easy to spell, it looks odd, and yet all it means is thinking out loud. Who'd want to do a thing like that, eh?

Language in Shakespeare Texts

Shakespeare's language can seem daunting — but it all boils down to looking at who says what.

Show you're aware of how Old it is

1) Shakespeare's plays are about 400 years old, so it's not surprising that we find the language a bit strange.
2) The humour is a bit different too — lots of the jokes are puns (words with double meanings). They also thought the idea of girls dressing up as boys was funny.

Be Specific when you write about Language

Think about what effect these things would have on the audience:

1) Imagery — look out for similes, metaphors and personification.

   E.g., in 'Othello', Iago uses lots of images of hell and the devil. This links him with evil.

2) Striking words and phrases — these are words that jump out at you.

   E.g., in 'Romeo and Juliet', Tybalt says "Drawn, and talk of peace! I hate the word, as I hate hell, all Montagues, and thee". This shows us how angry he is.

3) Humour — look out for puns and jokes in the text, and say what they show about the characters.

Look out for switches between Verse and Prose

Shakespeare's characters speak in a mixture of poetry and prose.

1) Most lines are written in blank verse. This has a regular rhythm but it doesn't rhyme.
2) It's grander than prose (see below), but any of the characters can speak in it.

> If music be the food of love, play on;
> Give me excess of it, that, surfeiting,
> The appetite may sicken, and so die.
> *Twelfth Night* Act 1 Scene 1

1) Rhyming verse is used at the beginning and ends of scenes or bits where a posh character is speaking or where a character is in love.
2) It makes the speech sound dramatic and impressive.

> From forth the fatal loins of these two foes
> A pair of star-cross'd lovers take their life,
> Whose misadventur'd piteous overthrows
> Doth with their death bury their parents' strife.
> *Romeo and Juliet* The Prologue

1) The rest is written in prose.
2) Prose is mainly (but not only) used for minor characters and funny bits.

> FESTE: Like a drowned man, a fool and a mad man:
> one draught above heat makes him a fool;
> *Twelfth Night* Act 1 Scene 5

Language — no phonecall would ever be the same without it...

When you write about a Shakespeare play, you'll need to choose quotes to back up the points you're making. So be on the look out for key bits of language you can use to support your ideas.

What You Have To Do

Poetry questions often follow the same pattern — learn how to answer them and you'll bag big marks.

Break the Question into Parts

When you're working out what to write about, underline the key words in the question so that they stand out.

This is the instruction.

This is the topic.

> Compare how feelings about relationships are shown in 'Praise Song for My Mother' and one other poem from 'Relationships'.
>
> Remember to compare:
> - the feelings in the texts
> - how these feelings are shown

You need to write about two poems to get a good grade.

The bullet points tell you what to write about.

You need to think about these Things

1. Your opinion and ideas about the poem.
2. How structure, form and language are used to show ideas and themes.
3. Similarities and differences between poems and their effect on the reader.

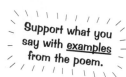

Support what you say with examples from the poem.

You'll Always have to write about Language

The question might ask you directly about language —

> Compare the poets' choice of language in 'Hour' and one other poem.

The question might be worded differently, but it still wants you to talk about language —

These all want you to write about the poet's use of language.

> Write about how the poets show these feelings to the reader.

> Write about the ways in which these ideas are presented.

The language, you say? — er, English, I think...

Make sure you follow the instructions in the question. If it says "Write about 'Wind' by Ted Hughes and one other poem", then just writing about 'Wind' will mean you miss out on marks.

What You Have To Do

Poetry can be tricky, but there are some things you can do in your essay to earn top marks.

Keep In Mind what the question is Asking

1) Use short quotes from the text to back up your points. Remember to comment on what they show.

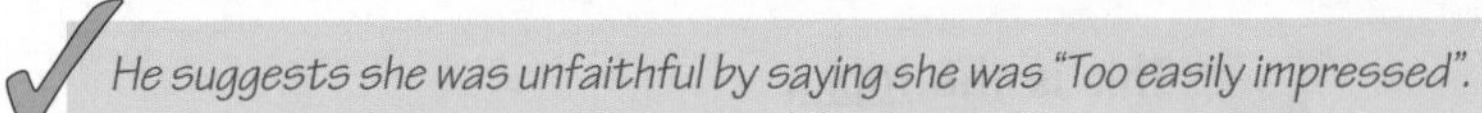

instead of

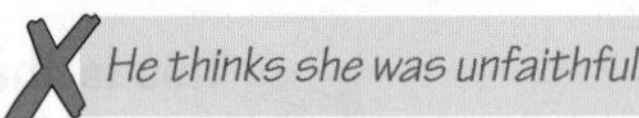

2) Make clear, definite statements.

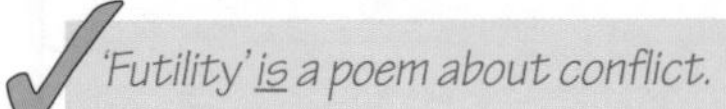

instead of

I think 'Futility' might be a poem about conflict.

You'll have to Compare different poems

Comparing means finding similarities and differences between two or more poems.

You could say something like:

In 'Sonnet 116', Shakespeare says that love doesn't change when beauty fades. However, in 'To His Coy Mistress', Marvell says that it's best to love before you become old and less attractive.

Show that you Understand what the poet is doing

1) You have to show that you can put yourself in the poet's place and understand what they're feeling.
2) You need to write about how the poet feels and how you think they want to make you feel.

Star-strewn... no. Rough-hewn... no. Darkling moon... hmm.
Oi, budge up. I need to put myself in your place.

Be Imaginative

1) Write about your own ideas about the poem, how it makes you feel and what you think it means.
2) Think about other ways that the poem could be interpreted (what else it could mean).
3) There's only one rule — you must back up your idea with a quote from the text.

Poems are like suitcases — you need to unpack them...

When you're comparing poems, it's important that you talk about similarities and differences between them — don't just write about one poem, then about the other. See p.51 for more on comparing.

Style and Structure in Poetry

Different structures and styles are used in different kinds of poem...

Learn the different Types of poem

There are different types or forms of poems. Writing about form is a good way to get marks.

Ballads — Ballads have a regular rhythm and tell a story. They often have four-line verses and a chorus.

Elegies — An elegy is written for someone who has died, and is usually quite slow and thoughtful.

Free Verse — Poems written in free verse have lines of uneven length that do not have to rhyme.

Sonnets — Sonnets are usually 14 lines long, with a regular rhyme scheme.

Write about Form and Structure

A poem's form is its physical features — for example the number of lines, rhyme and rhythm. Using these words to describe a poem's form makes you sound like you really know your stuff:

- A stanza is the proper word for a verse.
- A rhyming couplet is a pair of lines that rhyme.
- A tercet is a three-line stanza.
- A quatrain is a four-line stanza.

Structure is how the poet arranges the ideas or events in the poem to put them across most effectively.

For example in 'next to of course god america i' by E E Cummings, the final line shows that the speaker is addressing an audience, and is nervous. This makes the reader suspicious of the speaker.

Work out the Voice of the poem

1) First-person narration uses "I" and "me". It helps the reader understand the narrator's viewpoint, so it's often used for poems about personal things.

2) Third-person narration uses "he" and "she". Third-person narration can sound more detached than first-person narration, which makes the reader trust what the narrator's saying.

Free verse — the opposite of converse...

Some poems have forms that are easy to write about (e.g. sonnets). But you can write about any poem's form, even if it's to make the point that it doesn't have a regular one.

Words To Use When Writing About Poetry

Using technical words when you write about poetry will impress the examiner and get you better marks.

Using the Right Technical Words will get you marks

Don't use these words if you're not sure what they mean — here's a quick reminder for you...

Alliteration — When letters are repeated, usually at the beginning of words. → The greedy goat guzzled the grass

MORE GRASS NOW!

Assonance — When vowel sounds are repeated in the middle of words. → The mouldy goat only hoped to float

Onomatopoeia — When a word sounds like what it means. → Crash, Splat, Bang

Enjambment — When a sentence runs from one line of poetry into the next one (can help emphasise certain words). → The goat was alone for three hundred thousand years.

This line starts with 'hundred thousand' so the number really stands out.

Rhythm — The beats within each line (like music). Can be regular or irregular. →
The goat required a field of grass each day. (regular)
The goat was so hungry he stuffed his big fat ugly face. (irregular)

Pace — How quick/slow/clunky/graceful the words actually sound. → "The goat gambolled gracefully over the green green grass" has a faster pace than "The goat, which was young, climbed nimbly and gracefully up the craggy mountain."

Tone — What feeling the words are spoken with (e.g. anger, happiness, fear, etc...). →
"Only a goat would understand modern art today" (irony)
"If only I hadn't given in to the goat's commands" (regret)

If you're really stuck — write about goats...

Using the proper words for things will bag you extra marks in the exam, so it's worth learning them. There are some more useful words on p.50 — go back and make sure you remember them.

What You Have To Do

When you write about prose, you still need to talk about themes, characters and language...

Write a bit about When it was Written

1) You often have to show you know when the text was written, and what significance this has. There's more on how to do this further down this page.
2) Some books are set at the same time they were written in. Other books are set in a different time or place.
3) This means the author can write about present-day issues without criticising anyone directly.

George Orwell wrote Animal Farm in 1945. It tells the story of a bunch of pigs who take over a farm. It's not actually about pigs though — it's about events which took place around that time in Russia.

Show you Understand the Issues being dealt with

1) Texts can address social issues: 'Robin Hood' is concerned with poverty.

2) They can have historical themes: Different versions of 'Robin Hood' have different interpretations of the role the royal family played at that time.

3) They can have a moral message: 'Robin Hood' portrays theft and mugging as acceptable, if it's for a good cause.

Write in Detail

Most questions ask you to comment on how a writer has shown the reader things.

- Personality of a character
- Experiences of characters
- Attitudes of characters
- Conflicts between characters
- Message and meaning of the text as a whole

'Warning! This vehicle is reversing...' — always back up with a quote

If you notice something (about language, a character etc.) while you're reading a text, put it in your essay. It's good to be original, as long as it's relevant to the question and backed up with a quote.

What You Have To Do

The main thing is to read the question carefully, so you don't go barking up the wrong tree.

Questions about the Message can look daunting

This is the kind of question you might get:

Here's the topic you need to write about.

How is war presented in *'Lord of the Flies?'*

This is the message bit.

In questions about the message, you always need to write about what the writer is trying to say.

Golding suggests in *Lord of the Flies* that war is inevitable. We can tell this because...

Some questions ask about a Specific chunk of Text

Some questions will quote a page or so of one of your set texts and ask you a question about it.

...and now my hair is as thick as ever. Thank you CGP.

If you're answering a question on an extract, talk about these 3 things:

How is the extract relevant to the rest of the text?
Why is it important?
How are language, structure and form used in the extract?

You might have to write about Style

Some questions will ask you about the writing style.

Your answer will be about the usual style things (e.g. language, imagery, tone — see p.49). Remember — don't talk about these things as if they just happen by accident.

Let the examiner know that you understand it's all done by the writer.

The writer uses symbolism in this section to show us that...

The writer puts a bad joke at the bottom of each page to annoy the reader...

The examiners really want to know that you understand that stories are made up by real human beings. Quite silly, isn't it? You'd think they'd already have figured that one out themselves...

Writing About Writers

If you're asked how the writer shows the reader something, you'll need to know this stuff.

How does the writer put the text together?

How are the paragraphs structured? → In what order is information given to the reader?

What language have they used? → Why has the writer used one word instead of another? What have they left out?

Who is the narrator? → Why has the writer chosen to write from a certain viewpoint?

How has the writer used imagery? → What pictures has the writer created in your mind? Why have they done this?

Why does the writer choose one way over another?

It's what writing is all about — finding the best way to tell your story.
There's no right or wrong way to structure a book or use language — it's about using what's appropriate.

> Meera Syal uses Midlands dialect words in *Anita and Me*, which makes the book's main characters seem more real.

> Allan Stratton wrote *Chanda's Secrets* in the first person. This helps the reader to understand the viewpoint of Chandra, the main character.

What is the writer trying to do?

1) The examiner wants to know that you understand that short stories and novels have been thought up and written by the writer, and that the writer is trying to make you think in a particular way.
2) You can show that you are aware of this by referring to the writer. For example:

> In 'Paddy Clarke Ha Ha Ha', Roddy Doyle tells the story from Paddy's point of view.
> This means we see the behaviour and problems of the adult characters through a child's eyes.

I don't know what the writer's trying to do — he should explain better

It's tempting to think that the writer just sits down one day with a cup of tea and a chocolate digestive and starts writing whatever comes into their head, but it doesn't actually work like that.

Questions About Characters

Character questions come up a lot. You need to be able to write about characters confidently to do well.

Make sure you Prepare for character questions

Make revision notes on these things for the texts you're studying — then you'll be sorted for any exam question on characters. Not all of these will apply to all stories — pick the ones that fit best.

Why is a certain character important?

Think about how each character affects the plot and what would happen if they weren't there. E.g. in 'Of Mice and Men', would Lennie and George have achieved their dream if Curly's wife hadn't been living on the farm?.

Does the character change or learn something?

1) Characters often change over the course of a text. Think about whether their personality changes and whether their behaviour gets better or worse.
2) For example, in 'Lord of the Flies' Jack becomes more savage after he paints a mask on his face.
3) Also think about whether the character has learnt something that's changed their actions or opinions.

How does the writer reveal a character's personality?

1) Take a character and say whether the reader and the other characters see them and their experiences in the same way.
2) Think about whether the characters relate well to each other or whether they have differences in personality which affect the plot (e.g. Jack and Ralph in 'Lord of the Flies'). What is the writer trying to use these differences to show us?
3) You also need to consider whether a character has a particular point of view.

What does the writer want us to think about a character?

1) How do you feel about each character, e.g. do you like/sympathise with them? Think about why. You need to do this for the narrator, too.
2) Think about how the writer has used language and structure to make you feel that way and how it affects your view of the character.

The character changes from blue trousers to green tights

This isn't so you can pre-plan essays — that's ridiculous. You can't tell what the questions will be. It's just so that you're prepared and have the best possible chance in the exam.

Revision Summary

There are a fair few questions on this page, I'll give you that. But you haven't had any for the last couple of sections, so all's fair in love and er, revision. Make sure you do all these, check your answers against sections six, seven and eight, then go back and do any questions you got wrong again until you get them right. Ready?

Drama

1) Which three things do you need to show you understand when writing about a play?
2) What is stagecraft? What three things should you talk about to show that you appreciate it?
3) What is the name for a play that's supposed to make you laugh?
4) What is dialogue?
5) What are stage directions?
6) Are most lines in a Shakespeare play written in: a) rap b) blank verse c) prose?

Poetry

1) True or false? 'You'll always have to write about the language in poetry essays.'
2) Is it a good idea to be imaginative in a poetry essay? Why/why not?
3) How many lines does a sonnet usually have?
4) Stanza is the proper name for: a) a verse? b) a poem? c) a line? d) a word?
5) What is: a) pace? b) alliteration? c) enjambment?

Prose

1) Which of these things do you not need to look out for in a text?
   a) Social issues b) Snotty tissues c) Historical themes d) Moral Issues
2) What do you always need to do when answering a question about the message of a text?
3) What three things should you talk about when you're faced with an extract from a text?
4) If you're writing about how the writer has put the text together, what four things could you talk about?
5) How can you show that you're aware of what the writer's trying to do?
6) Write down five things about characters you could make revision notes on before the exam.

Make Your Writing Clear To Read

A big chunk of the marks for a writing exam question are for how you write, not what you write about.

Writing Well gets you a better grade

This is what you'll be marked on:

1) Standard English (see p.67)
Unless you're writing in the voice of a character, examiners will expect you to use Standard English. Don't slip into slang or local dialect, or you'll lose marks.

2) Punctuation (see p.68-70)
Punctuation is brilliant for making your writing smooth, clear and punchy — but only if you get it right. Make sure you know when to use commas, apostrophes etc.

3) Spelling and types of words (see p.72-74)
Your spelling needs to be pretty accurate if you want a good grade, and it also helps if you know how to use different types of words correctly.

4) Sentence types (see p.75)
Use a mixture of sentence structures — from short and simple to long and complex.

5) Using varied language (see p.76-77)
Use similes and metaphors when you're describing something, and make sure you use some interesting words too.

6) Paragraphs
Writing in paragraphs is very important for organising your writing into manageable sections.

Writing bad English don't get you nowhere...

If you learn the rules in this section and use them when you're writing, you won't go too far wrong. Make sure you check your work before you hand it in, so you can correct any obvious mistakes.

Standard English

The examiners want you to use Standard English, so you'll lose marks if you don't know how...

Use Standard English

1) People in different parts of Britain use different local words (dialect) that can be difficult for outsiders to understand.

Mad fur it
aye our kid!

2) Standard English avoids any dialect words and is understood by people all over the country.

Using Standard English means following some Simple Rules

1) Don't write the informal words you'd say when talking to your friends, e.g. 'OK', 'yeah'.
2) Don't use slang or local dialect words that some people might not understand.
3) Use correct spelling and grammar.
4) Don't use text speak.

Avoid these Common Mistakes

1) **RULE**: don't put the word '<u>them</u>' in front of names of objects — always use '<u>those</u>'.

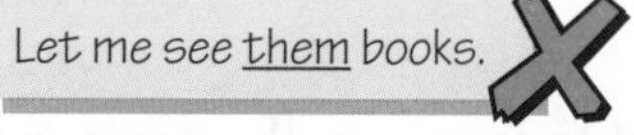

Let me see them books.

Let me see <u>those</u> books. ✓

2) **RULE**: '<u>who</u>' is used to talk about people. '<u>That</u>' or '<u>which</u>' is used for everything else.

King Lear had two daughters <u>who</u> lied to him.

Percy met a lion <u>that</u> did not kill him.
OR
Percy met a lion <u>which</u> did not kill him.

Either 'that' or 'which' is fine.

3) **RULE**: Don't write '<u>like</u>' when you mean '<u>as</u>'.

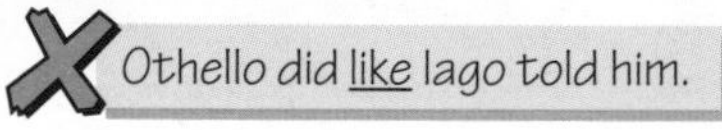

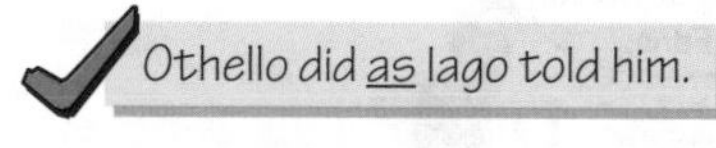

This sounds much better.

Use Standard to improve your standard...

Another thing the examiners, like, really hate is if you, like, keep using the word 'like' when you, like, don't need it. Only use informal language like this if it's suitable for a character's speech.

Punctuation

Punctuation isn't just there to make your essays look pretty — it's there for a reason...

Start and Finish your sentences correctly

Always start sentences with a capital letter. Sentences always end with either:

- a full stop — use these for most sentences.

- a question mark — use these if the sentence is asking a question.

- an exclamation mark — use these if you want your sentence to have a strong impact.

Use Commas to put Pauses in sentences

1) Commas separate the parts of long sentences to make the meaning clear.

In the valley below, the villages all seemed very small.

Without the comma, the sentence would begin 'in the valley below the villages'.

2) Commas are also used to break up the items in a list:

I bought onions, mushrooms, peppers and pasta.

3) Pairs of commas can be used to add extra information to the middle of sentences:

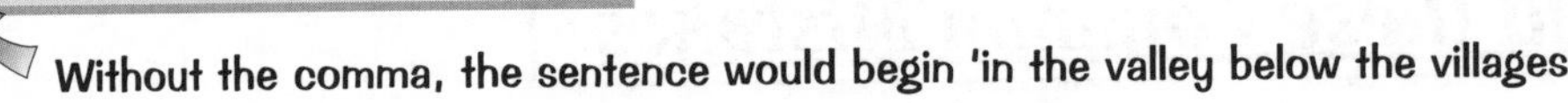

The twins, who had their blue wigs on, were eating seaweed.

comma comma

The sentence would still work without the bit in the middle.

You NEED to learn this stuff on punctuation — full stop...

lordy lordy just think how hard it would be to read something without punctuation it would drive you up the wall and it's the same for the examiners they can't stand it at all so use it I tell you

Apostrophes

Apostrophes can seem tricky, but they're not actually too difficult if you stick to a few simple rules...

Add 's to show Who Owns something

The dog belongs to Montel so you add an apostrophe + 's' to the name of the owner.

Montel's dog is less scary now.

There's a catch, though:

Its = something belongs to it.
Its doesn't follow the apostrophe rule.

The dog has had its dinner.

It gets a bit Tricky with Groups of People or Things

They found the killer eels' lair during the men's underwater race.

1) If it already ends in s, stick an apostrophe on the end but not an extra s.

2) Plural words that don't end in s, e.g. men, women and mice, follow the normal rule of apostrophe + 's'.

Apostrophes can show where there's a Missing Letter

1) You can shorten some pairs of words by sticking them together and cutting out letters.
2) You put an apostrophe to show where you've removed the letters from.

E.g. I am → I'm   The letter 'a' has been removed, so an apostrophe goes in its place.

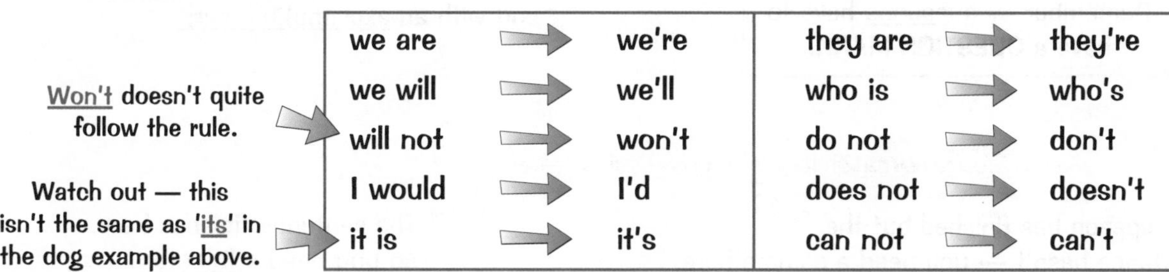

Won't doesn't quite follow the rule.

Watch out — this isn't the same as 'its' in the dog example above.

we are	→	we're	they are	→	they're
we will	→	we'll	who is	→	who's
will not	→	won't	do not	→	don't
I would	→	I'd	does not	→	doesn't
it is	→	it's	can not	→	can't

The horror, the horror — Apostrophe Now

And now, a word of warning — never, ever use an apostrophe to show that something's plural (for example: two banana's, five pear's). I know your greengrocer does it, but that doesn't make it right.

Speech Marks

You guessed it — speech marks are yet another thing the examiner will be looking out for.

Speech Marks show someone's Actually Speaking

Start of speech

End of speech

"You're going to lose that pretty hat," said Bob.

These are the words Bob said — they go in the quotation marks.

Always Start Speech with a Capital Letter

"Let's have a game of pogo-stick golf," said Claude.

Here's the capital letter.

The speech bit always begins with a capital letter — even if it isn't at the start of the sentence.

Doug asked, "Where's the nineteenth hole?"

"My pogo stick," Claude boasted, "is brand new."

If a speech is split into two sections, you don't need a capital letter at the start of the second section.

End speech with a Question Mark, Full Stop or Comma

"Who will fight me in a duel?" asked Louise.

Remember — questions have to have a QUESTION MARK.

Marco shouted, "I'm not afraid to fight!"

Marco's shouting, so this should end with an exclamation mark.

"You're no match for me," replied Louise bravely.

The speech has finished but the sentence hasn't — you need a comma here.

The sentence finishes here, so you need a full stop.

Unaccustomed as I am...

The punctuation rules might seem a bit tricky, but it's well worth learning them, because they're exactly the same when you're quoting from a text in a literature essay. Handy, eh?

Negatives

It's a page about negatives — deep breath, chin up and don't let it get you down.

'No' Isn't the only Negative word

The easiest way to make a phrase negative is to add 'no' or 'not' (or by adding -n't to a word, see p.69).

Positive sentence:

My aubergines are rotten.

Negative sentence:

My aubergines are not rotten.

Don't use Double Negatives

I don't want no aubergine. **REALLY MEANS** I do want some aubergine.

Two negative words in the same phrase will make it positive. You should use only one negative at a time.

WARNING: Never use a quadruple negative.

The word None has different meanings

1) 'None' can cause problems, because it has different meanings.

It can mean 'not one': None of the students passed the test.

It can also mean 'not any': I want an aubergine, but there are none left.

2) The main thing you need to remember is that 'none' should not be used with other negative words:

He has not got none. 

He has none. ✓

Stop being so negative — it's not that bad...

I'll pass on some advice my granpappy gave to me — he sat me down on his knee one day and said, "Now don't you go using no double negatives, you hear." My granpappy was a wise man.

Spelling

Some spelling mistakes are really common — luckily this page tells you how to avoid making them.

Don't confuse Different words that Sound the Same

Two words that sound similar can mean different things. Here are some common examples to look out for...

1) affect/effect

1) Affect means 'to influence something'. → Burning fossil fuels affects Earth's climate.
2) An effect is the result of an action. → The effect of burning fossil fuels is global warming.

2) there/their/they're

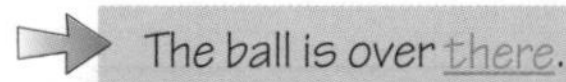

1) There is used to talk about place. → The ball is over there.
2) Their shows that someone owns something. → Their dog bit me!
3) They're is the short form of 'they are'. → They're my favourite shoes.

Never come between a dog and his favourite shoes.

3) where/were/wear

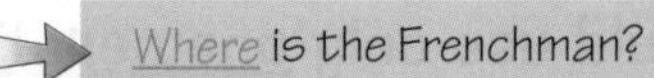

1) Where is used to talk about place. → Where is the Frenchman?
2) Were is a past tense of the verb 'to be'. → They were hidden behind a statue.
3) Wear is what you do with clothes, shoes etc. → He wants to wear his new bow tie.

4) your/you're

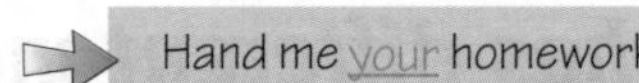

1) Your means something that belongs to you. → Hand me your homework.
2) You're is the short form of 'you are'. → You're not allowed to eat that in here.

Watch out for these Common Spelling Mistakes

1) Words with a silent 'h' — you don't say it, but you must write it: e.g. chemistry.
2) Words written with 'ph' and pronounced with an 'f' sound: e.g. graph or philosophy.
3) Words with an 'i' next to an 'e': e.g. hygiene or believe.
4) Words where the endings change when they're made plural: e.g. babies not babys.

Get your spelling write...

You need to know how to spell the names of writers and the title of any books, poems and plays you're studying. Take a look at p.50, p.60 and p.90 for more words that you should learn how to spell.

Nouns, Verbs, Adverbs and Adjectives

You need to know the proper names for the different types of words, so get your learning hat on.

A Noun is a Person, Place or Thing

There are four kinds of noun:

1) 'Proper' names (towns, people, months etc.). E.g. Gloria, Sunday, Texas.
2) Groups of people or things, e.g. class, pack, squad.
3) Names of other everyday things, e.g. hedge, hair, woman.
4) Words for ideas, e.g. truth, beauty, fear.

Proper names always have capital letters.

Verbs are 'Doing' or 'Being' words

'Doing' words

riding thinks ate belches

'Doing' words tell you what's happening in a sentence.

'Being' words

Today was good.

I am happy.

'Being' words tell you how something is or was or will be.

Adjectives describe Things and People

Global warming is bad.

Too boring — zero marks alert!

Global warming is a serious and worrying issue.

Much better — the adjectives will impress the examiner.

Adverbs describe How an Action is done

The tree fell, missing my leg.

Boring — the verbs have been left plain.

The tree fell suddenly, narrowly missing my leg.

The adverbs make the sentence more exciting.

I always turn off the TV during the adverbs...

Use different verbs, adjectives and adverbs to spice up your writing. It'll get you more marks in the exam, and help to make you more attractive to the opposite sex*. *Well, it won't make you less attractive, anyway.

Using Verbs in Sentences

The message of this page is that your sentences need to make sense. Simple, but very important.

Every sentence needs a Verb

1) Verbs are 'doing' words or 'being' words (see p.73) — and every sentence needs to have one.
2) The form of the verb changes depending on when the action takes place.

In the past

I was the world's first snail-tamer.

In the future

I will be the world's first snail-tamer.

These are both 'being' words — but they're in different tenses.

Make sure you use the Right Form of the verb

1) Every verb describes what someone (or something) is doing (or being).
2) If there's only one person doing something, use the singular form of the verb.
3) If there's more than one person doing something, use the plural form of the verb.
4) When you're writing a verb in a sentence, say it out loud. Decide whether it sounds right or not.

NO! This sounds wrong. 'They' means more than one person, so the subject is plural.

They was eating mouse sandwiches. ✗

Much better — that sounds right and it makes sense too.

They were eating mouse sandwiches. ✓

Don't change When Things Happen in your writing by Mistake

This is in the past. Another past verb.

As they tried to get the sail up, they could hear distant splashes — then they see a canoe.

This one's wrong — it's in the present when it should be past (i.e. 'they saw a canoe').

I was singular — then I tried speed dating...

If you don't follow these three rules, then you're asking for trouble. Worse than that... if you don't follow these three rules, you're mad.

Remember to include a verb in every sentence you write.

Sentences

If you really want to wow the examiner, you'll need to use different types of sentence...

Vary the Style of your sentences

Using different sentence types will make your writing more interesting. Here are some types you could try:

Simple sentences are good for emphasising important points.  My cat likes Mexican food.

You could add another part to the sentence and join it to the first part using a word like and or but.  My cat likes Mexican food, but he won't eat curry.

You could also try adding another part in the middle of the sentence.  My cat, who has a wonky tail, likes Mexican food.

Start your sentences in Different Ways

Your writing will be pretty boring if all your sentences start with the same words. For example:

There was a chill in the air as Jo walked towards the house. There was nobody around. There was a big oak door and Jo knocked on it. There was a scream from inside the house.

It's much more interesting if you vary the way you start sentences:

There was a chill in the air as Jo walked towards the house. Nobody was around. Jo knocked on the big oak door. A scream came from inside the house.

Write your sentences in a Logical Order

If you write your sentences in the wrong order, your work will be hard to understand. For example:

Harry went flying and landed in a silage pit. Unfortunately it was faster than him, and it headbutted him with all its force. Harry turned to run as the angry bull charged towards him.

What's happening isn't clear, because the sentences aren't in the right order. The order should be:

1. Harry turned to run as the angry bull charged towards him.  2. Unfortunately it was faster than he was, and it headbutted him with all its force.  3. Harry went flying and landed in a silage pit.

Simple sentences rule, although complex ones are better.

It can also be really effective to include the occasional question in your writing — it can help the reader feel more involved and keep them interested in what they're reading.

Writing Varied Sentences

When you're describing something you need to paint a picture in your reader's head — here's how.

Describe things by Comparing them to Other Things

Comparing your subject to something else helps readers to imagine it.
There are three different ways of comparing:

1) Using less than, more than, the least, the most...

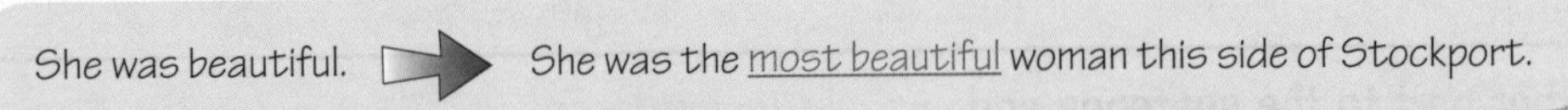

She was beautiful.
She was the most beautiful woman this side of Stockport.

2) You can also say something is more than or the most by adding "er" or "est" to the end, e.g. smaller, kindest. But do this INSTEAD of using "more than" or "most".

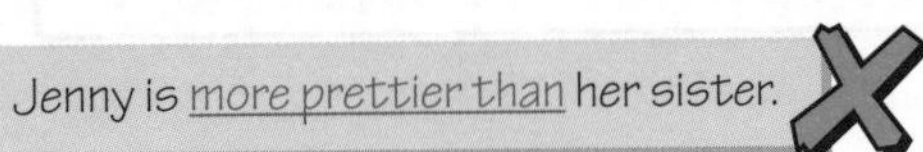

Jenny is prettier than her sister. 

3) Using similes (say that one thing is like another). You can use the words "like" or "as":

My fingers were like blocks of ice.

Beth felt as happy as a hippo in a mud pool.

Metaphors can create Strong Images

1) A metaphor describes one thing as if it is something else.
2) Metaphors can have a very powerful effect if used carefully.

Leela cried so hard that a river flowed down her cheeks.

There wasn't really a river flowing down Leela's cheeks, but the language creates a strong visual image.

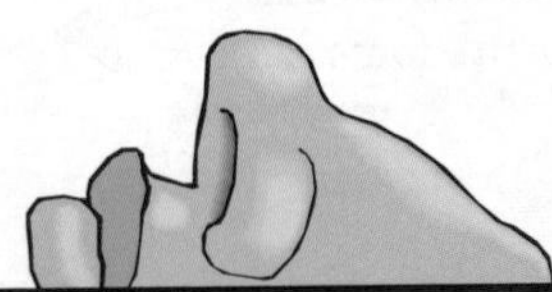

Dry land, dead ahead!

Jenny? I know her well — I've metaphor times...

Using similes and metaphors will make the examiners see your work as an oasis of loveliness in the lonely desert of tedious, unimaginative essays that they all too often have to mark.

Writing Varied Sentences

Using lots of different words makes your writing more interesting, which is what the examiner wants...

Use Different Words for the Same Thing

Don't use the same word all the time — especially vague ones like "nice" or "weird".

I went to a nice Indian restaurant last night. The waiters were nice to us. I had a nice curry.

This isn't going to score you many points because it's so boring.

This is loads better. Using lots of different adjectives paints a more interesting picture.

I went to a fantastic Indian restaurant last night. The waiters were friendly to us. I had a delicious curry.

It's the same with verbs (doing or being words)...

I ran to the post box with a letter, then I ran to the shop for some chocolate. After that I ran home so I wasn't late for tea.

I ran to the post box with a letter, then I hurried to the shop for some chocolate. Finally I raced home so I wasn't late for tea.

Fancy Words impress the examiner

Using different words is good, but if you're after top marks, try using different and clever words.

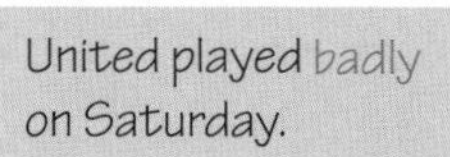

United played dreadfully on Saturday.

The referee made some very stupid decisions.

The referee made some incredibly moronic decisions.

Use loooonnnggg wooooorrdddsssss...

You shouldn't use long, fancy words all the time — that'd sound daft. But you'll get extra marks if you throw them in every now and then. So, invest in a dictionary and learn some crazy new words.

Revision Summary

There's loads of stuff to take on board here. Browse back over the section, and when you feel confident, try these questions. Check on any you got wrong, then have another go. It'll take a little while — but you need to be able to sail through the questions like a knife through butter...

1) True or false: Standard English uses lots of regional dialect words.
2) Rewrite this sentence in Standard English — "Nellie really loves them cream buns."
3) Give two types of punctuation that can be used to end a sentence.
4) Insert commas in this sentence so that it makes sense:
   "However the book was written well so I enjoyed it."
5) Correct the mistakes in these sentences:
   a) My sisters hamster has looked very happy since I brushed it's coat.
   b) Its nice to see a smile on its little face.
6) Cut out letters and replace them with apostrophes. The first one is done for you.
   a) I will not = I won't b) can not c) I would d) it is e) they are
7) What type of punctuation do you need to use when someone's speaking?
8) Which of these is a negative sentence?
   a) I don't know the answer. b) I know the answer.
9) What effect does the double negative have in this sentence — "I don't see no lake"?
10) Which of these statements is correct?
    a) We where going to a fancy party.
    b) I decided to wear my birthday suit.
    c) I don't know were that idea came from.
11) Give three examples of nouns.
12) Find the adverb in this sentence — "I glanced quickly behind me."
13) Rewrite this sentence as if it happened in the past — "I am a great disco dancer."
14) What's wrong with this sentence — "The children only eats sausages"?
15) True or false: It's good to start all your sentences with the same word.
16) What three letters could you add to the word "cold" to make it mean "most cold"?
17) Is the following sentence a simile or a metaphor — "He was as charming as a sewer rat"?
18) Write down three words that mean "bad".

How to Study Spoken Language

This section is about real-life, genuine, home-grown, actual speech — the way people really talk.

Listen Carefully to what People Say

If you're doing WJEC in Wales you won't have to study spoken language.

1) The language you use changes depending on what situation you're in and who you're talking to. For example, you call your headmaster 'sir' rather than 'mate'.
2) Pragmatics are hidden or suggested meanings. E.g. you might say to a friend "This maths homework's impossible", when what you mean is "Can you help me with it?".
3) When you say things like 'yeah' or 'mm' to show someone you're listening, it's called feedback.

Spoken Language is different from Written Language

When people speak naturally, their speech has non-fluency features. Here are some examples:

1) Fillers (e.g. 'er', 'um') — these fill gaps while the speaker thinks of what they want to say.
2) False starts — where the speaker starts saying one thing, then changes their mind.
3) Repetition — people repeat words a lot in unplanned speech, e.g. 'I'm never never going'.
4) Interruption/overlap — people sometimes talk over each other.

Here are some other things you'll hear in real-life speech:

1) Missing words — e.g. 'want to come out' instead of 'do you want to come out'.
2) Slurring words together — e.g. 'gonna' instead of 'going to'.
3) Small talk — phrases that don't have much meaning, e.g. 'Hi, how are you?', or 'Bye'.
4) 'Vague' language — e.g. saying 'sort of', 'like' or 'lots'.
5) Turn-taking — speakers taking it in turns to lead the conversation.

Listen out for How People Speak

1) Stress is when you emphasise certain words to change the meaning of the sentence.
2) Tone of voice can change the meaning of what you say, e.g. make it playful or sarcastic.
3) Volume can affect meaning — e.g. loudness might show anger, excitement or confidence.

Spoken Language — a bit like written language, only louder...

Blimey. That's an awful lot to think about, but don't worry — it'll make a lot more sense when you start looking at some data and have some sort of context to relate it all to. Trust me, it will.

Social Attitudes to Spoken Language

Some people have strong feelings about the way people speak...

Accents and Dialects can be Regional or Social

An accent is just how you say words.

A dialect is the actual words you use.

1) People with different accents pronounce the same words in different ways. E.g. people from London sound different from people from Liverpool.
2) Regional accents are different depending on which part of the country the speaker's from.
3) A social accent is the result of someone's class or background.

Different Groups Speak Differently from each other

Different groups of people use different language when they're talking together. For example, middle-aged lawyers speak differently from teenagers.

1) Sharing group language gives a group an identity — people use it to fit in.
2) Some people think women use more Standard English, and swear and interrupt less than men.
3) Men often use more non-standard grammar and have stronger regional accents.

Idiolect is the Unique way a Person speaks

1) Your individual way of speaking is called your idiolect. Everyone's idiolect is different.
2) It's influenced by the accent and dialect in places you've lived and the people you've spent time with (i.e. your social background).

Some people think that Non-Standard English is 'Wrong'

1) People have strong opinions about different varieties of English.
2) Some people think that standard English is 'correct' and other forms of English are wrong.

But — the type of English that's appropriate to use depends on what you're doing. For example, you'd probably use more slang in an informal chat than in a job interview.

Spare me the lect-ure...

So the basic message to take away from this page is that not everyone speaks in the same way. Wow, I could have told you that. Wait, I think I just did... Oh well, just get on and learn it anyway.

Spoken Genres

Public talk (speeches) and talk in the media is written down to be spoken out loud.

Public Talk is Written to be Spoken

'Public talk' means things like political speeches, or a presentation in a school assembly.
It's written for a specific purpose, and uses some of these techniques:

1) Public speakers use Standard English to make their speech sound serious and impressive.
2) They might use pauses, stress and tone of voice to give the speech meaning.
3) Individual public speakers and interviewers have their own unique ways of talking, so you could also look at specific speech patterns — e.g. the way someone phrases questions.

You could look at Spoken Language in the Media

1) Things like news reports are planned beforehand to make sure they make sense. The presenters on these programmes use Standard English.
2) Language in the media can also be spontaneous (unplanned) — e.g. talk on reality shows.
3) Radio plays and TV soaps and dramas try to sound like real-life talk. The actors often have regional accents and might interrupt each other to make it seem realistic.

Scripted speech is never exactly like real-life talk. If it was then it wouldn't flow, and the audience might miss bits because people were talking at the same time.

Radio Language is Different from TV Language

1) TV language has pictures, gestures and facial expressions to help get the meaning across.
2) On the radio, everything has to be explained using words.
3) Radio presenters have to fill all the silences, so they don't pause very much.

Silence is golden — except if you're talking on the radio...

Spoken language is a funny thing — it's surprisingly hard to mimic the everyday, real-life speech that we hear all the time. Instead, all the talk you hear on the TV and radio is a bit more formal.

Multi-Modal Talk

Multi-modal language is like a mixture of written and spoken language.

Modes are different Types of language

1) Written modes include written texts like novels, letters, recipes etc.
2) Spoken modes are things like informal conversations, radio broadcasts and speeches.
3) Multi-modal talk means written conversations that contain elements of spoken language — e.g. using smileys to show what your facial expression would be if you were speaking.

Technology has had a big impact on the amount of multi-modal talk that people use.
In electronic texts like emails, people's writing tends to be less formal and a lot more like speech.

Text Messages and Online Conversations are Multi-Modal

You can have conversations with people via text message or online instant messaging.
These conversations are multi-modal because they can contain lots of 'text speak'.

1) Text speak contains features of spoken language — things like saying 'hi' or 'bye'.
2) Words in text speak often have letters missed out or replaced with numbers or symbols because it's quicker and cheaper than typing words out in full, e.g.:

gona be in ldn this wknd if ur around?wud b gr8 2 catch up

3) Online conversation can work like spoken conversation — you take turns and make it clear when it's the other person's go, e.g. by asking them a question.

ROFLMAO

Some people think Text Speak is 'Bad' English

1) Some people say text speak is hard to understand, and stops people being able to spell properly.
2) Others think it's useful for texts or online chat, but not for other situations.
3) You could argue that language always changes, so text speak is just a natural progression.

Multi-modal? I prefer America's Next Top Modal...

It seems like a lot to take in, but a lot of this stuff you'll know all about from experience anyway — it's just a case of learning some fancy terms for things you do every day.

Data

You'll probably be given data for your Spoken Language study. Here's a heads up on what to expect.

Your Data is the spoken language you'll be Analysing

There are all sorts of different types of data that you could get for your controlled assessment:

1) Transcripts of real-life talk (more on transcripts below).
2) Transcripts of audio clips (e.g. a radio show or a TV interview).
3) Text messages or online chat conversations.
4) Scripted language (e.g. a radio advert or public speech).
5) Newspaper articles, or other material that shows people's attitudes to spoken language.

Transcripts look like this

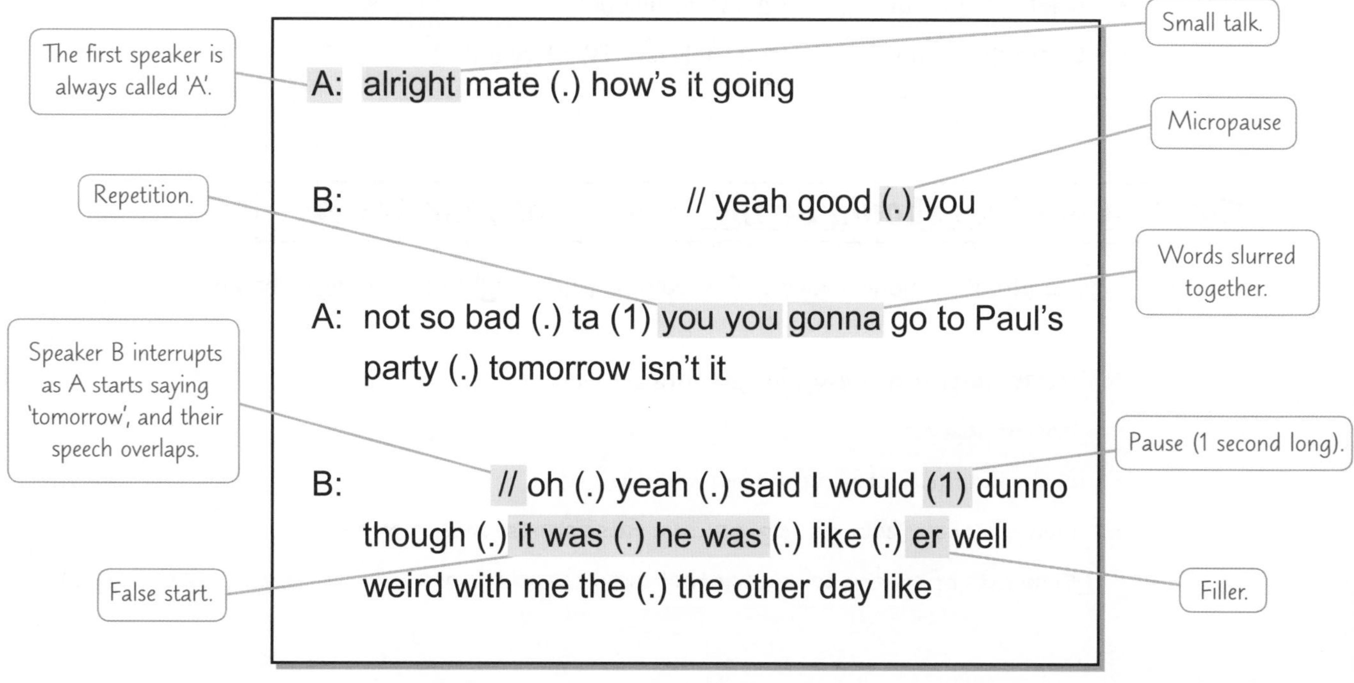

A: alright mate (.) how's it going
B: // yeah good (.) you
A: not so bad (.) ta (1) you you gonna go to Paul's party (.) tomorrow isn't it
B: // oh (.) yeah (.) said I would (1) dunno though (.) it was (.) he was (.) like (.) er well weird with me the (.) the other day like
The first speaker is always called 'A'.
Repetition.
Speaker B interrupts as A starts saying 'tomorrow', and their speech overlaps.
False start.
Small talk.
Micropause
Words slurred together.
Pause (1 second long).
Filler.

Key

(.) = micropause (less than 1 second)

(2) = a pause showing the number of seconds it lasts (so this one's 2 seconds long).

Interruptions or overlap are shown using the symbol // at the point where someone's interrupted.

28 days' data — now that is a scary thought...

If you're given a transcript, it might not look exactly the same as the one above, but it will be similar. Don't forget that numbers or full stops in brackets are there instead of punctuation.

Writing Up Your Spoken Language Study

Now you know what kind of data you're likely to get, here's how to write about it really well.

Think about How you'll Structure your Work

A three-part structure is best:

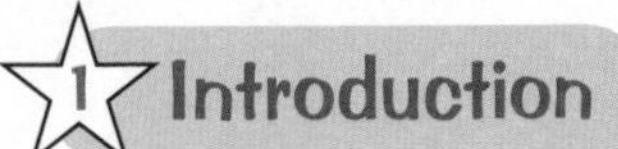

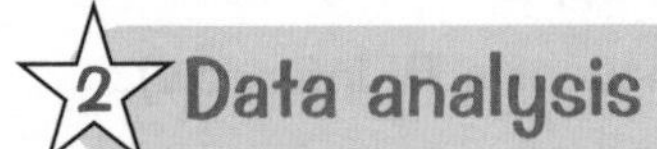

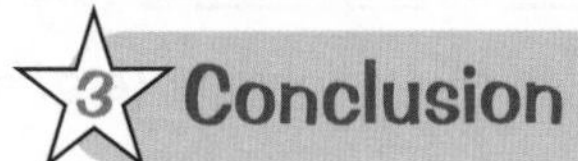

When you give in your final essay, make sure you also hand in your data and notes.

Make Sure you have a Good Introduction

In your introduction you need to say something about:

- what kind of spoken language you're looking at.
- what features of it you're going to discuss.
- where the data is from — e.g. 'this is a TV interview'.

The Data Analysis should be the Main Bit of your Answer

Use paragraphs to structure your answer. For example, you might have paragraphs about:

- Vocabulary (e.g. slang, jargon, dialect words)
- Accent/dialect
- Grammar (e.g. standard or non-standard)
- Non-fluency features (e.g. pauses, false starts, interruption)
- Elements of spoken language that aren't words (e.g. loudness, stress, tone of voice)

Finish with a Conclusion

1) In your last paragraph, you should sum up what you've found out.
2) Remember to refer back to the question — say what your data shows and how it answers the question.
3) Then you'll be as happy as this lady.

Blah blah pun — something something joke...

You get the idea. If you can get a good structure from the start, your answer should fall effortlessly into place. The controlled assessment can be a gold mine of marks if you plan properly.

Speaking and Listening

You'll be assessed on different types of speaking and listening skills — read on to find out more.

There are Three Main Types of task

The three types of task are:

1) individual presentation
2) discussion
3) role play

Teachers are on the lookout for certain things in the speaking and listening tasks:

- Put across your points clearly in a style suitable for the situation and audience.
- Listen to what other people say, ask questions and make sensible comments.
- Play the part of a character without slipping out of the role.

Remember the CAP Rule when you speak

The CAP Rule stands for Courtesy, Audience, Purpose

1 COURTESY

Be polite at all times, especially when other people are doing their tasks. If you're nice to them, they'll be on your side when you're speaking.

OI, YOU LOT! Shut up and listen to this!

2 AUDIENCE

Change your speech to suit your audience. You might be speaking to a big group, so you'll have to keep people interested.

3 PURPOSE

Get your information across as clearly as possible. Keep your speech well-organised and to the point.

This is the Speaking Clock — the time now is 8.02...

You should use Standard English for these tasks — unless you're playing a character who has a regional dialect. Just remember — CAP: Courtesy, Audience, Purpose — and you'll be on track to do well.

Speaking and Listening

Speaking to an audience is different from chatting to your mates — here's what you need to know.

Use Standard English

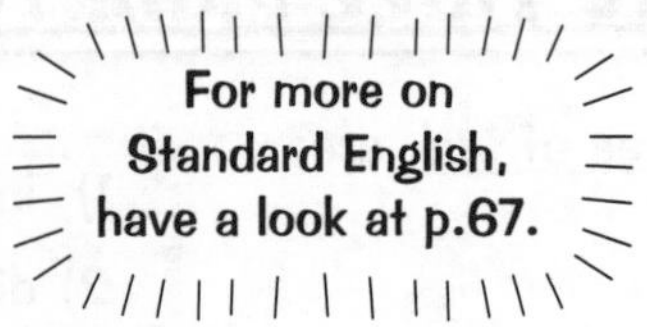

For more on
Standard English,
have a look at p.67.

1) Speak in Standard English. That doesn't mean you have to hide your accent — just speak clearly.
2) Don't use slang. You'll lose marks.

Be Clear

1) Don't mumble. Speak up and look around the room while you're talking.
2) Make sure what you're saying has a clear structure, and isn't just a load of unconnected points.
3) Write notes to remind you of your main points, but don't write out every single word you want to say.

Work out what your most important piece of information is. Think carefully about where you put it in your speech.

Don't repeat yourself. Once you've made a point, move on.

Choose your words carefully so they're suitable for your audience.

Listen Carefully and Be Polite

When other people are talking, you have to show you're listening and that you understand what they're saying.

- Don't interrupt the speaker.
- Ask questions about what the speaker has said. If you don't understand something, politely ask them to explain it.
- When you give feedback on someone else's talk, mention the good things that they said.
- If you don't agree with the speaker's opinion then politely explain why you think they're wrong.
- Only criticise what the speaker said, not how they said it — e.g. if they sounded nervous, don't mention it.

You must speak properly — like what I does...

You can be a bit less formal in a discussion, but when you're giving a talk you should only use Standard English. Whatever you do, don't do it in Cockney rhyming slang. I did that once and it was a disaster.

Speaking and Listening — Individual Presentation

Three pages on the different tasks you might have to do — lucky you. First up, a presentation...

You might have to do a Presentation

1) You may have to do a presentation — it could be on your own or in a group.
2) If you're allowed to choose your own topic, choose one that interests you.
3) At the end of your presentation you'll have to answer questions about it.

This is the Type of Task you might be given

Here are some examples of the type of presentation you could do:

- Talk to your class about a subject you're interested in — e.g. your favourite sport or your last holiday.
- You could be interviewed — e.g. for your school magazine.
- You could interview someone else — e.g. talk to your grandparents about their memories.
- Make a case arguing for or against something that concerns you — e.g. club nights for under-18s.

You can use slides, pictures, etc. to back up your points.

Plan your presentation

1) Plan your presentation in detail to make sure that it gets your point across clearly.
2) Think about who you're talking to — and how much they know about your subject.
3) Use Standard English, interesting language (see p.30) and a wide range of words to get top marks.

I'd like to interview Hugh Jackman...

Your presentation might be given to the whole class, to a small group, or to entirely different people. You'll find out who your audience is in advance, so you'll be able to make sure your talk is suitable.

Speaking and Listening — Discussion

For a discussion task you have to listen to other people and get your own views across.

You might have to have a Discussion with Other People

1) In a discussion, you have to listen to other people's arguments and try to persuade them that your point of view is right.
2) You'll probably work in groups for this task — pairs, threes, fours or a bigger group.
3) You need to think about both sides of the issue you're discussing.
4) When other people comment on what you say, listen to their opinions and answer their questions.
5) You need to ask questions as well. When someone else is talking, pay attention so you can join in.

This is the Type of Task you might be given

Here are some examples of the type of discussion you could do:

- With a partner, give a presentation to your class, then answer questions about it.
- Discuss a topic that affects you — e.g. whether your school should have more recycling bins.
- Try to solve a local issue — e.g. car parking in a busy part of town.
- Discuss one of the texts you're studying — e.g. who's to blame for the deaths in Romeo and Juliet.

Back Up your Ideas to get Good Marks

1) Think carefully about the points you're making and make sure that you can back them up.
2) Give your own ideas and encourage others to share theirs.
3) Use Standard English, interesting language (see p.30) and a wide range of words.

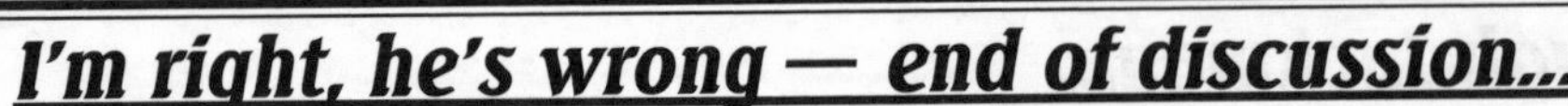

I'm right, he's wrong — end of discussion...

The most important part of this task is listening to other people and showing you've understood what they've said by asking them questions. You also need to help keep the discussion moving.

Speaking and Listening — Role Play

Role play — putting on a silly voice and pretending to be someone else. Now you're talking.

You get to do some Drama

1) For a role play task you have to play a character and present their point of view.
2) Role play is like acting — you have to imagine you're the character and act like them.
3) You'll probably work in pairs, but for some tasks you might work in a group or on your own.
4) Your teacher will set you a task — it might be related to a text you're studying.
5) You're not allowed to use a script.

This is the Type of Task you might be given

Here are some examples of the type of role play you might have to do:

- Explain the actions of a character from one of the texts you've been studying — e.g. Jack talking about why he acted the way he did in 'Lord of the Flies'.
- Carry out an interview with a character from one of the texts you've studied — e.g. a policeman interviewing Friar Lawrence in 'Romeo and Juliet'.
- Carry out an interview about an important issue — e.g. knife crime.
- Discuss a current news item as if you were a newsreader.

You have to Stay in Character to get Good Marks

1) To get high marks in this task, you need to keep your role play interesting and entertaining.
2) Give lots of thought to how your character would act as well as what they would say.
3) Think about the situation, and make sure your language is appropriate. For example, if you're playing a politician, you shouldn't use slang.
4) Stay in character all the way through.
5) Use Standard English, interesting language (see p.30) and a wide range of words.

Umm, Kev? You can come out of character now... It's hometime.

No sniggering at the back...

You might be allowed notes or prompts for some tasks. Think carefully about what you will find most helpful during the task and write the notes out neatly so you can actually read them.

[The end.]

Commonly Misspelled Words

Here is a list of the most common words that people spell wrongly. Cross off the ones you can already spell and then learn the rest. If you don't you'll just be throwing marks away.

absence
accelerate
acceptable
accident
accommodate
accurate
achieve
acknowledge
acquaintance
across
address
aeroplane
aisle
amount
anxious
argue
argument
assistant
association
athlete
authorise
autumn
awkward
basically
beautiful
beginning
believe
biscuit
build
business
cease
ceiling
chaos
cheque
chief
chimney
choose
chose
college
colourful
column
coming
commit
completely
criticism
deceive
decision

definitely
describe
despair
desperate
develop
disappear
disappoint
double
dread
eerie
efficient
embarrass
environment
equipment
exaggerate
exceed
except
excitement
exercise
existence
experience
extremely
familiar
fascinate
February
fiery
finally
financial
foreign
forty
forward
friend
gorgeous
government
grammar
grateful
happened
height
holiday
humorous
humour
ignorant
imaginary
immediately
independent
innocent
intelligent

interrupt
irrelevant
irritable
jewellery
judge
judgement
knock
knowledge
labour
laughter
leisure
library
lightening (making lighter)
lightning (and thunder)
likeable
maintain
marriage
murmur
necessary
neighbour
niece
ninety
noticeable
occasionally
occur
occurrence
panic
panicked
personal
philosophy
piece
playwright
possess
pursue
quay
questionnaire
queue
reassure
receive
receipt
recommend
relief
repetition
resource
restaurant
rhyme

rhythm
ridiculous
secretary
scenery
schedule
seize
separate
similar
sincere
skilful
solemn
sophisticated
souvenir
stationary (not moving)
stationery (equipment)
style
succeed
successful
surprise
symbol
temporary
theatre
therefore
thieves
thorough
tomorrow
tongue
truly
twelfth
typical
tyre
umbrella
unnecessary
unnoticed
until
vague
vegetable
vicious
weather (sun and rain)
Wednesday
weight
weird
whether (if)
which
whole (entire)
wreck
yacht

Index

Index